Ethnic Chicago
Cookbook

Ethnic-Inspired Recipes
from the Pages of the

Edited by
Carol Mighton Haddix

CB

CONTEMPORARY BOOKS

Maxwell Street Market, circa 1905.

Library of Congress Cataloging-in-Publication Data

Ethnic Chicago cookbook : ethnic-inspired recipes from the pages of
    the Chicago tribune / edited by Carol Mighton Haddix.
        p.   cm.
     Includes index.
     ISBN 0-8092-2848-3
     1. Cookery, International.   2. Cookery—Illinois—Chicago.
 I. Mighton Haddix, Carol.   II. Chicago tribune.
 TX725.A1E845   1998
 641.59—dc21   98-21865
                                          CIP

Caramelized Fennel Soup: Reprinted with the permission of Scribner, a division of Simon & Schuster, from *Patricia Wells at Home in Provence: Recipes Inspired by Her Farmhouse in Provence* by Patricia Wells. Copyright 1996 by Patricia Wells.

Zucchini and Cheese Patties and *Baked Savory Manti:* Copyright 1997 by Ghillie Basan, from *Classical Turkish Cooking* by Ghillie Basan. Reprinted by permission of St. Martin's Press, Inc.

The Real Salad Niçoise: From *Flavors of the Riviera* by Colman Andrews, copyright 1996 by Colman Andrews. Used by permission of Bantam Books, a division of Bantam Doubleday Dell Publishing Group, Inc.

Belgian Meatballs Braised in Beer: Excerpted from Ruth Van Waerebeek's *Everybody Eats Well in Belgium Cookbook*, copyright 1996 by Ruth Van Waerrebeek. Used by permission of Workman Publishing Co., Inc., New York. All rights reserved.

Spaghetti with Butter and Cheese: From *Essentials of Classic Italian Cooking* by Marcella Hazan. Copyright 1992 by Marcella Hazan. Reprinted by permission of Alfred A. Knopf, Inc.

Cover design by Mary Lockwood
Cover photographs: Tribune Photos by Bill Hogan (top left), Bob Fila (top center), and John Dziekan (top right); photograph courtesy of *Giordanos*, Chicago (bottom)
Interior design by Mary Lockwood
Interior photographs: Chicago Historical Society (ICHi-19155) by Barnes-Crosby (pages ii–iii). Tribune Photos by Donald Casper (page x); Tribune Photos by Walter Kale (page 1); Tribune Photos by Bob Fila (pages xii, 43, 63, 85, 145, 169, 181, 221) Inserts: Additional Tribune Photos by Bob Fila, Bill Hogan, James F. Quinn

Published by Contemporary Books
A division of NTC/Contemporary Publishing Group, Inc.
4255 West Touhy Avenue, Lincolnwood (Chicago), Illinois 60646-1975 U.S.A.
Copyright © 1999 by the Chicago Tribune Company
Printed in the United States of America
International Standard Book Number: 0-8092-2848-3
98 99 00 01 02 03 QP 18 17 16 15 14 13 12 11 10 9 8 7 6 5 4 3 2

Contents

Soups   43

Salads   63

Side Dishes

Breads

Acknowledgments

Special thanks go to the cooks, chefs, restaurateurs, authors, and readers who have contributed recipes through the years to the *Chicago Tribune* "Good Eating" and "Home" sections and to the *Chicago Tribune Magazine*.

Andy Badeker, Renee Enna, Kristin Eddy, and William Rice generously contributed the recipe introductions and helped compile the ethnic market list.

Photographers Bob Fila, James F. Quinn, Tony Berardi, Bill Hogan, and John Dziekan have shot beautiful photographs of even the simplest of dishes. Test Kitchen director Alicia Tessling and food stylist Joan Moravek have tested recipes and created works of art from simple ingredients.

Thanks to JeanMarie Brownson for her fine recipe editing.

For all of the nutrition information with each recipe, dietitians Jo Ellen Shield and Mary Mullen deserve credit.

Thanks also goes to all of the *Chicago Tribune*'s Editorial Information Center staff members who combed the files for these recipes and photographs: Linda Balek, Kemper Kirkpatrick, Mary Wilson, Judy Marriott, Joe Pete, Alan Peters, and Larry Underwood. Rosemary Johnson deserves credit for tracking down recipe permissions.

And for encouragement and letting it all happen, appreciation goes to editors Howard Tyner, Gerould Kern, Janet Franz, Denise Joyce, and Joe Leonard.

Deep-dish pizza at Pizzeria Uno

Introduction

Chicago is a cultural crossroads. At last count, more than eighty different ethnic groups are represented in the city and its suburbs.

Since the first wave of traders and pioneers swept into this area in the late 1700s, Chicago has been multiethnic: French traders, British soldiers, and the native Potowatomis who coined the city's name, *chicagu*, from their word for the wild onions so abundant in the swampy terrain.

Then came the Irish, escaping their potato famine, and the Germans. By the early 1900s, Chicago had welcomed influxes of Greeks, Poles, Italians, Jews from Eastern Europe, and Chinese. As the century progressed, immigration continued from ever-widening parts of the world: the Caribbean, Mexico, Hungary, Korea, the Philippines, Thailand, and Vietnam, to name just a few. The newcomers carried their food traditions with them. Many of them opened restaurants and food shops to serve their people.

Longtime residents soon discovered these foods and relished the fresh, unusual—and often inexpensive—fare. The city became one of neighborhoods, each often revolving around an ethnic population. Many of these enclaves still are in evidence today, complete with their produce stands, bakeries, butchers, and restaurants.

Through the years, the pages of the *Chicago Tribune* have mirrored the changing face of the city's inhabitants. And no more so than in the food pages, where recipes for ethnic dishes began creeping into print, tucked between staid Midwestern standards.

Making pierogi in Ukranian Village

By the end of World War II, America's interest in cuisines from around the world was piqued. Soldiers returning from France, Italy, and the South Pacific came home with a taste for "exotic" fare. And Americans began traveling, falling in love with the foods they found, and trying to duplicate them back home, making do when necessary with American ingredients. Soon, more imported foods arrived, specialty shops stocked them, and even basic supermarkets started devoting shelf space to foods from around the world—tropical fruits from Central America or Asian greens such as mizuna or seaweed.

Fusing Cuisines

In the last five to ten years, we have seen a gradual shift in the way ethnic recipes have appeared in the food pages of the *Chicago Tribune*. More and more, international influences have been slipping into mainstream American dishes. Plain chicken salad becomes Chinese chicken salad with the addition of water chestnuts and cilantro. Burgers become Asian with lemongrass or sesame flavors. And a classic porterhouse takes a Mexican turn when guajillo chilies are added to the pan juices.

It's called fusion cuisine—a sometimes subtle, sometimes not so subtle, mix of American ingredients or techniques with those from other lands. Chefs have led the way, applying American or French techniques to Asian or Latin ingredients or vice versa, mixing classic preparations such as poached fish teamed with a stir-fried vegetable topping.

The idea of this worldwide mix-and-match cuisine no longer seems strange to home cooks. It's an adventurous way to add a touch of spice to everyday meals. We've become familiar with what used to be exotic ingredients. Our pantries boast curry mixes, couscous, arborio rice, and coconut milk.

Our refrigerators hold cilantro, mangoes, fresh tortillas, and bok choy.

Your Cooking Adventure

The recipes in this book reflect this increasing sophistication in home cooking. While beginning cooks will find many simple, quick dishes that can be prepared from ordinary supermarket ingredients, adventurous cooks will appreciate the more exotic recipes.

Once you have stocked the pantry, freezer, and refrigerator with some basic ingredients, fusion cooking is easy. You'll learn to freeze leftover coconut milk to use in small amounts to flavor any stew or soup. Chipotle chilies from a can also can be frozen whole or pureed and tossed in small amounts into a weeknight meat loaf. Asian flavored oils keep well in the refrigerator. Frozen gnocchi and tortellini make great instant meals when combined with chicken broth and herbs.

For more unusual ingredients, check out the ethnic markets listed in the Appendix. Part of the fun of cooking ethnic dishes comes in exploring these shops. They are a window into a culture. And they are the first step to great, adventuresome meals that bring the world to your table. We hope you agree.

Nutrition Information

The nutrition content of recipes in this book has been calculated by Mary Mullen and Jo Ellen Shield, registered dietitians.

Because of variations in ingredients and measurements, the numbers are approximations. This is especially true for dishes that involve marinades; in most cases we have assumed that one-fourth of marinade ingredients end up in the finished dish.

When a recipe gives a range in the amount of an ingredient, the smaller amount is used.

Analyses do not include optional ingredients, garnishes, fat used to grease pans, or suggested accompaniments unless specific amounts are given.

Salt is figured only if a recipe calls for a specific amount. Salt added to cooking water is not included. Broth or stock is considered to be the salted variety unless otherwise specified.

Ethnic Chicago
Cookbook

Appetizers and Light Dishes

Grilled Vietnamese delicacies, Argyle Street

Eggplant Hummus

Preparation time: 20 minutes
Cooking time: 10 minutes
Chilling time: Several hours
Yield: 12 appetizer servings

Nutrition information per serving:

Calories	81
Fat	6 g
Cholesterol	0 mg
Sodium	140 mg
Carbohydrate	7 g
Protein	2 g

NOTE

For larger, older eggplant, peel and salt it before cooking it. Salt the cut surfaces, put it in a colander, and weight it down with a heavy object for 30 minutes, allowing the bitter liquid to drain out. Before using, rinse it off with cold water and blot dry with paper towels.

Tahini is a sesame seed paste, available in the ethnic sections of supermarkets and Middle Eastern markets.

This addictive variation on hummus, a thick Middle Eastern sauce typically made with mashed chickpeas, was created by Chicago Tribune *columnist Abby Mandel. Make it a day ahead for the best flavor. Serve the hummus as a dip with toasted pita triangles, thin baguette toasts, crackers, or raw vegetables.*

1 medium eggplant, peeled and cut into 1-inch cubes, see Note
1 cup fresh parsley leaves
⅓ cup fresh lemon juice
½ cup tahini, see Note
1 large green onion, cut into small pieces
1 medium clove garlic, minced
¾ teaspoon salt
Ground red pepper to taste

1. Put eggplant into a wide-bottomed steamer over hot water. Steam, covered, until soft, about 10 minutes. Transfer to paper towels; blot dry with towels.

2. Transfer eggplant to a food processor fitted with a metal blade. Add remaining ingredients. Process until very smooth. Adjust seasonings (be moderate because mixture picks up flavor as it stands). Chill several hours, preferably overnight. Before serving, mix well; adjust tahini, lemon juice, and seasonings. Serve chilled.

Salsa in a Snap

This quick-fix salsa is great on a nachos platter. Layer it cold on tortilla chips covered with melted cheese, refried beans, and guacamole. It also works as a warm sauce for chicken breasts or pork chops.

1 28-ounce can Italian-style whole plum tomatoes
2 jalapeño peppers, boiled 5 minutes and chopped (but not seeded)
1 small onion, chopped
¼ cup chopped cilantro
1 clove garlic, minced
Salt to taste

1. Place tomatoes in a saucepan; heat to boiling. Reserve 1 teaspoon each of the chopped jalapeños and onion.

2. Place tomatoes and remaining ingredients except for reserved jalapeño and onion in a blender or food processor fitted with a metal blade. Pulse until blended. Stir in reserved jalapeño and onion. Serve cold or warm.

Preparation time: 15 minutes
Yield: 3½ cups

Nutrition information per 2 cups:

Calories	15
Fat	0 g
Cholesterol	0 mg
Sodium	95 mg
Carbohydrate	4 g
Protein	1 g

Fresh Tomatillo Sauce

Preparation time: 15 minutes
Yield: About 2½ cups

Nutrition information per
½ cup:

Calories	30
Fat	1 g
Cholesterol	0 mg
Sodium	235 mg
Carbohydrate	6 g
Protein	1 g

The tomatillo is a tangy fruit that looks like a miniature green tomato with a paper wrapper. Popular in Mexican cooking, it is often used in fresh salsas. The natural wrapper must be removed before eating. Many Mexican preparations like this one use a molcajete, a kind of mortar and pestle in which foods are ground. Serve this with tortilla chips or as a sauce over grilled fish or chicken.

8 tomatillos, papery covering removed
2 cloves garlic
½ teaspoon salt
1 medium white onion, chopped
1 serrano chili, seeded and minced
½ cup cilantro leaves

1. Heat enough water to cover tomatillos to a boil in a medium saucepan; add tomatillos. Cook 1 minute. Drain; rinse in cold water. Set aside.

2. Grind garlic with salt in a mortar or in a blender container; do not puree. Add onion and chili; process to chop lightly. Add cilantro and blanched tomatillos, a few at a time; process to chop lightly. Adjust seasoning.

Feta Cheese Spread

This tangy spread—tyrosalata in Greek—comes from
Papagus Greek Taverna, located in the River North
neighborhood in Chicago. Use it with toasted pita triangles or
Greek sesame bread as part of a weekend party with friends.

Preparation time: 10 minutes

Yield: About 2½ cups

1 pound imported feta cheese
1 3-ounce package cream cheese, softened
1 tablespoon half-and-half
1 tablespoon lemon juice
1 teaspoon white pepper
3 tablespoons olive oil

Nutrition information per
tablespoon:

Calories	45
Fat	4 g
Cholesterol	13 mg
Sodium	135 mg
Carbohydrate	1 g
Protein	2 g

1. Break up feta into a mixing bowl. Add cream cheese; beat
   to mix thoroughly. Add half-and-half, lemon juice, and
   pepper. Beat to mix thoroughly.

2. Pour oil into cheese mixture in a thin stream, beating constantly. Taste and adjust seasoning as desired. Transfer to
   a bowl or deep plate.

Spiced Pita Chips

Preparation time: 10 minutes
Cooking time: 8 minutes
Yield: 4 servings

Nutrition information per serving:

Calories	105
Fat	3 g
Cholesterol	5 mg
Sodium	295 mg
Carbohydrate	18 g
Protein	3 g

Former Chicago Tribune *food writer Pat Dailey created these quick homemade chips to accompany a meal of spring vegetable ragout with couscous. They are a good way to use up leftover pita.*

2 pita bread rounds
2 teaspoons unsalted butter, softened
½ small onion, sliced paper-thin
¼ teaspoon crushed red pepper flakes
¼ teaspoon cumin seeds
¼ teaspoon salt
⅛ teaspoon poppy seeds
Pinch caraway seeds

1. Heat oven to 400°F. Butter one side of each bread round; cut into quarters. Arrange on a baking sheet. Place several slices of onion on each. Combine remaining ingredients in a small bowl; sprinkle over each bread piece. Bake until crisp, 6 to 8 minutes.

Bruschetta

Put day-old slices of Italian bread to good use in this snack from the Chicago Tribune's "Fast Food" column. Consider adding chopped fresh tomatoes when they are in season, or ribbons of sliced fresh basil.

Preparation time: 10 minutes
Cooking time: 3 minutes
Yield: 4 servings

2 tablespoons extra-virgin olive oil
½ teaspoon tomato paste
½ teaspoon dried basil
½ teaspoon fresh lemon juice
1 clove garlic, minced
Pinch crushed red pepper flakes
6 slices Italian bread, about ½ inch thick
1 tablespoon grated Romano cheese, preferably imported

Nutrition information per serving:

Calories	189
Fat	9 g
Cholesterol	2 mg
Sodium	287 mg
Carbohydrate	23 g
Protein	5 g

1. Place broiler rack 8 inches from heat source; heat broiler. Mix oil, tomato paste, basil, lemon juice, garlic, and red pepper flakes in a small bowl.

2. Spread mixture on each bread slice. Sprinkle with cheese. Broil just until bread is hot, 2 to 3 minutes.

Asian Pork and Crab Meatballs

Preparation time: 30 minutes

Cooking time: 5 minutes per
  batch

Yield: About 25 meatballs

Meatballs can be found in cuisines the world over. This Asian version is just one of the many ethnic takes. It makes a good appetizer to team with sparkling wine, according to Chicago Tribune *food and wine columnist William Rice. He likes to serve the meatballs with a sauce made of four parts rice vinegar and one part sesame oil.*

Nutrition information per meatball:

Calories	55
Fat	4 g
Cholesterol	13 mg
Sodium	70 mg
Carbohydrate	0 g
Protein	4 g

¾ pound lean ground pork
⅓ pound fresh or frozen crabmeat, defrosted, cartilage
  removed
1 tablespoon tamari (aged soy sauce)
¼ cup minced green onions
2 teaspoons minced gingerroot
¼ teaspoon hot pepper sauce
Vegetable oil

1. Combine pork, crabmeat, tamari, onions, ginger, and hot pepper sauce in a large bowl. Mix well. Form into 1-inch meatballs. (This may be done several hours ahead. Cover balls tightly and refrigerate until 15 minutes before cooking.)

2. Pour oil into a large skillet to a depth of 1 inch; heat over medium heat to about 350°F. Fry meatballs in batches, turning often, until browned, about 5 minutes. Drain on paper towels.

Veal Meatballs with Bay Leaves

These fragrant, unusual meatballs wrapped in bay leaves are from Evanston, Illinois, cooking teacher Maria Battaglia, who says fresh lemon leaves are a good choice, too.

Preparation time: 30 minutes
Cooking time: 6 to 8 minutes
Yield: 4 servings

1 pound ground veal
1 large egg
½ cup grated caciocavallo or Parmesan cheese
½ cup dried bread crumbs
¼ cup chopped fresh flat-leaf parsley
¼ cup chopped fresh basil leaves
Salt to taste
Freshly ground black pepper to taste
2 to 4 tablespoons olive oil, extra-virgin preferred
24 dried bay leaves, soaked 15 minutes in warm water

Nutrition information per serving:

Calories	300
Fat	18 g
Cholesterol	130 mg
Sodium	415 mg
Carbohydrate	10 g
Protein	25 g

1. Prepare grill or broiler. Soak thin wooden skewers in water 15 minutes. Mix veal, egg, cheese, bread crumbs, parsley, basil, salt, and pepper in a medium bowl. Shape mixture into meatballs the width of a bay leaf. (There should be about 24.)

2. Pour oil into a shallow dish; roll meatballs around in oil until lightly coated. Wrap 1 bay leaf around each meatball; thread onto skewers, about 4 meatballs per skewer.

3. Grill meatballs over a medium charcoal fire or broil, 6 inches from heat source, turning once, until cooked through, 6 to 8 minutes total. Remove from skewers to serving platter; discard bay leaves. Serve with toothpicks.

Satay with Creamy Peanut Dipping Sauce

Preparation time: 45 minutes

Marinating time: 30 minutes
or more

Cooking time: 4 to 5 minutes

Yield: 20 skewers

Nutrition information per skewer (chicken with 1 tablespoon dipping sauce):

Calories	110
Fat	8 g
Cholesterol	16 mg
Sodium	155 mg
Carbohydrate	4 g
Protein	7 g

Satay, skewers of seasoned meat and fish grilled over a charcoal fire and served with a dipping sauce, are found throughout Asia. Though food cooked on skewers, such as shish kebab, is found all over the world, certain characteristics are unique to satays: They are marinated and served with a sauce containing chili, spices, and usually ground peanuts, garlic, and onion. This recipe comes from the late cooking teacher Peter Kump.

Marinade and Meat

⅓ cup canola or safflower oil

⅓ cup packed cilantro, stems included

¼ cup fresh lime juice

¼ cup tamari (aged soy sauce)

1 piece peeled gingerroot, about 1 inch

8 medium cloves garlic, smashed

1 tablespoon plus 1½ teaspoons sugar

1 tablespoon ground cumin

1 small dry red chili or 1 tablespoon red pepper flakes

1 pound boneless, skinless chicken breasts, trimmed flank steak, pork tenderloin, or leg or loin of lamb, cut into 1-inch cubes

Dipping Sauce

1 14-ounce can unsweetened coconut milk

1⅓ cups peanut butter

½ cup whipping cream

2 tablespoons soy sauce

Juice of 1 lime

4 cloves garlic, peeled

1 piece gingerroot, about 2 inches, peeled and roughly chopped

2 tablespoons sugar

1 teaspoon crushed red pepper flakes

½ teaspoon ground red pepper

½ teaspoon ground coriander
½ teaspoon ground cumin

1. Soak 20 6-inch wooden skewers in water for 20 minutes. For the marinade, combine oil, cilantro, lime juice, tamari, ginger, garlic, sugar, cumin, and chili in a blender or a food processor fitted with a metal blade. Blend until cilantro and chili pepper are finely chopped. (Marinade can be made up to two days in advance and refrigerated. Bring to room temperature; stir well before using.) Add meat; marinate at room temperature 30 minutes or refrigerated 2 to 5 hours. Bring to room temperature before cooking.

2. For dipping sauce, mix all ingredients in a blender or a food processor fitted with a metal blade. Puree until smooth. Set aside.

3. Place broiler rack 4 inches from heat source; heat broiler. Or prepare grill, placing grill rack 3 inches above heat source. Place 4 to 5 meat cubes on each skewer. Arrange as many skewers as will make a single layer on broiler pan or on grill. Broil or grill until just cooked through, turning once or twice, 4 to 5 minutes. Repeat with remaining skewers. Serve with dipping sauce.

Cheese Squares

Preparation time: 20 minutes

Chilling time: 30 minutes

Cooking time: 15 minutes

Yield: 7 dozen

Nutrition information per square:

Calories	85
Fat	6 g
Cholesterol	25 mg
Sodium	35 mg
Carbohydrate	6 g
Protein	2 g

Restaurateur Ivan Kenessey shared this rich pastry appetizer from Hungary with readers of the Chicago Tribune *in a 1990 story about Hungarian Easter. The squares can be made up to a week in advance and stored in an airtight container.*

1 pound (4 sticks) unsalted butter, softened and cut into chunks

2¾ cups cake flour

2¼ cups all-purpose flour

¾ cup plus 1 tablespoon whipping cream

3 large egg yolks plus 1 whole large egg

1½ cups grated Parmesan cheese

1. Combine butter, flours, cream, egg yolks, and ¾ cup Parmesan in the bowl of an electric mixer. Beat on slow speed, gradually increasing to medium speed until a ball of dough forms. Gather dough together; flatten between 2 sheets of waxed paper; refrigerate until firm, about 30 minutes.

2. Turn dough out onto a floured surface. Roll out into a ¼-inch-thick rectangle with a floured rolling pin. Transfer dough to freezer for about 5 minutes to allow dough to firm up.

3. Heat oven to 350°F. Return dough to work surface. Beat whole egg; brush over top of dough. Sprinkle remaining ¾ cup Parmesan evenly over surface. Cut into 1½-inch squares. Transfer squares to ungreased cookie sheet(s), leaving ¼ inch between squares. Bake until golden, about 15 minutes. Transfer to a cooling rack; cool completely.

Zucchini and Cheese Patties

These spicy vegetable patties (kabak mucveri), *adapted from* Classic Turkish Cooking, *by Ghillie Basan, often are served hot with thick yogurt and garlic as a first course or as a side dish with lamb kebabs.*

3 large, firm zucchini, unpeeled and grated
Pinch of salt
3 tablespoons olive oil
1 large onion, chopped
4 cloves garlic, crushed with salt
3 eggs
3 tablespoons all-purpose flour
½ pound feta cheese, crumbled
1 tablespoon fresh dill, roughly chopped
1 tablespoon fresh parsley, roughly chopped
1 tablespoon fresh mint, roughly chopped
½ teaspoon sweet paprika
½ teaspoon ground red pepper
Freshly ground black pepper to taste
Vegetable oil for frying

Preparation time: 15 minutes
Cooking time: 15 minutes
Yield: 8 servings

Nutrition information per serving:

Calories	240
Fat	20 g
Cholesterol	95 mg
Sodium	340 mg
Carbohydrate	9 g
Protein	8 g

1. Sprinkle grated zucchini with salt; set aside 5 minutes. Squeeze out excess moisture. Heat olive oil in a shallow skillet; add zucchini, onion, and garlic and cook until lightly colored, about 5 minutes.

2. Beat eggs with flour in a large bowl until smooth. Add cheese, herbs, paprika, and red pepper. Stir in vegetable mixture; season with salt and black pepper.

3. Heat enough vegetable oil in a large skillet to cover bottom. Drop a spoonful or two of zucchini mixture into the skillet for each patty; fry until golden brown, 2 to 3 minutes. Turn over and cook 2 to 3 minutes. Drain on paper towels; serve hot.

Garden Vegetable Tempura

Preparation time: 15 minutes

Cooking time: 1 to 2 minutes
    per batch

Yield: 4 servings

Nutrition information per
serving:

Calories	430
Fat	17 g
Cholesterol	105 mg
Sodium	75 mg
Carbohydrate	59 g
Protein	11 g

When the Japanese deep-fry food, it tends to be shrimp and assorted vegetables encased in the lightest of batters, according to freelance food writer Andrew Schloss. He recommends serving the tempura pieces right out of the fryer with a mild dipping sauce such as plain soy sauce or soy sauce mixed with chopped ginger or green onions. To save time, buy the vegetables already cut up at the supermarket salad bar.

½ pound broccoli
½ pound cauliflower
½ pound carrots
2 large egg yolks
2 cups ice water
2 cups sifted flour
Peanut oil for frying
Soy sauce for dipping

1. Break broccoli and cauliflower into small florets. Cut carrots into matchstick pieces. Blanch all vegetables in boiling water, 1 minute. Plunge into a bowl of ice water to stop the cooking process; dry well.

2. For the batter, mix yolks and ice water in a medium bowl until well blended. Add flour all at once; mix until most flour has been moistened but mixture is still lumpy.

3. Heat several inches of oil to 375°F in a deep-sided heavy pan or wok. Dip vegetables into batter; drop 3 to 4 pieces into hot oil; fry until lightly browned, 1 to 2 minutes. Drain on a paper towel. Keep warm. Repeat with remaining vegetables. Serve with soy sauce for dipping.

Potato Latkes

These Jewish potato pancakes are an essential part of the annual Hanukkah celebrations. Serve with sour cream or applesauce for the finishing touch.

Preparation time: 40 minutes
Cooking time: 30 minutes
Yield: 8 servings

4 large Idaho baking potatoes, peeled
1 medium onion
2 large eggs, beaten
3 tablespoons all-purpose flour
1 teaspoon salt or to taste
½ teaspoon baking powder
¼ teaspoon freshly ground pepper or to taste
Vegetable oil for frying
Sour cream and/or applesauce

Nutrition information per serving:

Calories	190
Fat	11 g
Cholesterol	55 mg
Sodium	340 mg
Carbohydrate	21 g
Protein	4 g

1. Shred potatoes and onion in a food processor with a shredder blade or with a four-sided grater. Place in a colander; press out as much liquid as possible. Pat dry with a paper towel. Put potato mixture into a large bowl. Stir in eggs, flour, salt, baking powder, and pepper; mix well.

2. Pour enough oil into a large, deep skillet to lightly coat the bottom. Heat oil over medium heat until hot but not smoking. Cook 2 heaping tablespoons potato mixture per latke until golden brown on one side, about 2 to 3 minutes. Turn over and cook until brown; about 2 to 3 minutes.

3. Remove from pan; place on paper towels to absorb excess oil. Repeat to fry all the mixture, adding oil to the pan as needed. Serve warm with sour cream and/or applesauce.

Fresh Tomato Tart

Preparation time: 45 minutes

Cooking time: 55 minutes

Yield: 8 appetizer servings

Nutrition information per serving:

Calories	500
Fat	33 g
Cholesterol	35 mg
Sodium	735 mg
Carbohydrate	34 g
Protein	19 g

Potluck recipes, the mainstay of community gatherings and picnics, reflect America's melting-pot tastes. This recipe from Janice Sachen of Evanston, Illinois, was the second-place winner in the Chicago Tribune "Good Eating" section's Lucky Pot Contest in 1996. It works well at any potluck or for more formal parties, and is best when made with very ripe plum tomatoes.

Pastry

2 cups all-purpose flour

1 teaspoon salt

¾ cup cold vegetable shortening

½ cup ice water

Filling

¼ cup Dijon mustard

1 pound mozzarella cheese, thinly sliced or grated

10 medium plum tomatoes, thinly sliced

2 large cloves garlic, minced

2 tablespoons olive oil

2 teaspoons thinly sliced fresh basil leaves

1. Heat oven to 375°F. For the pastry, put flour and salt into a large bowl. Add shortening; use a pastry blender to cut into flour until it resembles coarse crumbs. Add water; toss gently with a fork until the mixture combines into a ball. Let rest 15 minutes.

2. Place the dough on a floured surface. Using a floured rolling pin, roll the dough into a circle large enough to fit a 10- or 11-inch tart pan with a removable bottom. Fit the dough into the pan; trim off excess dough. Pierce the bottom in several places with a fork. Bake until lightly colored, about 15 minutes. Cool on a wire rack.

3. Brush the bottom of the cooled pastry evenly with mustard. Cover mustard with cheese. Arrange tomato slices on cheese. Sprinkle with garlic and olive oil. Bake until crust is nicely browned, about 40 minutes. Sprinkle with basil. Let stand about 10 minutes; cut into wedges. Serve warm or at room temperature.

Cabbage Pierogi

Preparation time: 1 hour
Chilling time: 30 minutes
Baking time: 15 minutes
Yield: About 2 dozen pierogi

Nutrition information per
pierogi:

Calories	150
Fat	8 g
Cholesterol	40 mg
Sodium	185 mg
Carbohydrate	17 g
Protein	3 g

*These stuffed dumplings have their origin in eastern Europe, but
they are an old favorite in the Midwest. These pierogi, from the
late Lincolnshire, Illinois, caterer Marion Mandeltort, can be
assembled and refrigerated on a greased baking pan a day in
advance. About 15 to 20 minutes before they are to be served,
brush them with the egg wash and bake them.*

Dough
3½ cups all-purpose flour
½ cup (1 stick) unsalted butter, chilled and cut into
　　small pieces
1 teaspoon baking powder
½ teaspoon salt
2 large eggs
1 cup sour cream

Filling
2 tablespoons vegetable oil
2 carrots, peeled and finely slivered
½ head small cabbage, finely shredded
4 green onions, minced
1 tablespoon dried dill
1 teaspoon salt
1 teaspoon pepper
1 teaspoon sugar
1 tablespoon sour cream
1 egg yolk mixed with 1 tablespoon water

1. For the dough, put 3¼ cups flour and the butter, baking powder, and salt in a food processor fitted with a metal blade. Process until thoroughly blended. Add eggs and sour cream; process just until dough gathers. (If mixing by hand, put flour, baking powder, and salt into a bowl; cut butter in with two knives or a pastry blender until the mixture resembles coarse crumbs.) Remove dough from processor; knead in remaining ¼ cup flour. Shape dough into a flat round cake and wrap it in plastic wrap. Chill 30 minutes or until ready to use.

2. For the filling, heat vegetable oil in a large skillet. Add carrots, cabbage, green onions, dill, salt, pepper, and sugar. Cook over low heat until vegetables are slightly wilted but not mushy, about 10 minutes. Remove from heat; stir in sour cream. Taste for seasoning. The flavor should be strong, as it dissipates somewhat during baking.

3. Heat oven to 400°F. Roll pastry out on a lightly floured surface to ⅛-inch thickness. Cut pastry into rounds, using a 3-inch biscuit cutter. Put 1 teaspoon filling in the center of each round; fold dough over filling into a half circle, sealing the edges together with fork tines. Pierce the top of each pierogi with the fork.

4. Arrange on an ungreased baking sheet. Brush each pierogi with egg yolk and water mixture. Bake until lightly browned, about 15 minutes.

Siberian Meat Dumplings

Preparation time: 1 hour
Standing time: 30 minutes
Cooking time: 10 minutes
Yield: About 70 dumplings

Nutrition information per dumpling:

Calories	45
Fat	2 g
Cholesterol	10 mg
Sodium	40 mg
Carbohydrate	4 g
Protein	2 g

NOTE

Dumplings can be frozen before cooking. Place on a baking sheet; cover with aluminum foil or plastic wrap; place in freezer until frozen. Transfer to a plastic freezer bag. To cook the frozen dumplings, add them to boiling water and cook for 6 to 7 minutes.

What tapas are to the Spanish and dim sum is to the Cantonese, zakuska is to the Russians and residents of many of the republics of the former Soviet Union. Zakuska is defined as hors d'oeuvres or small bites. These addictive dumplings, pelmeni, adapted from a recipe by Chicagoans George and Valerie Samutin, are a Siberian specialty. A traditional item on the zakuska table, they often are dressed with vinegar, sour cream, and dill.

3 cups all-purpose flour
1 teaspoon salt
1 large egg
¾ cup cold water
¾ pound ground beef
½ pound ground pork
2 onions, finely chopped
1 cup crushed ice
Salt to taste
Freshly ground black pepper to taste
1 large egg white, lightly beaten
¼ cup (½ stick) unsalted butter, melted
Sour cream mixed with chopped fresh dill and/or white
    vinegar to taste, optional

1. Combine flour and salt in a food processor fitted with a metal blade. With the motor running, add egg through the feed tube. Pour in ¾ cup cold water in a slow, steady stream, just until the dough forms a ball around the blade (add additional water if needed). Transfer the dough to a floured surface; knead until smooth, about 2 minutes. Cover with a towel; let stand 30 minutes. Combine beef, pork, onions, crushed ice, salt, and pepper in a large bowl, stirring until mixed.

2. Divide dough in half; shape into two balls. Keep one ball covered with the towel. Roll out dough on a floured surface with a floured rolling pin to about 1/16 inch thick, making sure it does not tear. With a cookie cutter or glass, cut out 2½-inch circles.

3. Heat 6 quarts salted water to a boil in a large pot over high heat. Place 1 teaspoon meat filling toward the bottom of one dough circle. Brush the edges of the circle with egg white. Fold the empty half of the dough over the filling to form a semicircle. Press the edges firmly together with the tines of a fork to seal. Fold the two ends of the semicircle firmly together over the filled portion (like a tortellini); press against dumpling. Boil the dumpling 4 to 5 minutes; taste filling for seasoning. Add more salt and pepper to meat mixture if desired.

4. Fill and shape the remaining rounds, arranging the dumplings on a lightly floured baking sheet, about 1 inch apart. Roll out the remaining dough; cut, fill, and shape dumplings.

5. Gently add half of the dumplings to the boiling water; cook, stirring occasionally, until the dumplings rise to the surface and are cooked through, about 4 to 5 minutes. Remove to a colander with a slotted spoon to drain. Repeat with the remaining dumplings. Transfer to a deep serving bowl; toss with melted butter. Serve with sour cream, if desired.

Baked Savory Manti

Preparation time: 35 minutes
Cooking time: 40 minutes
Yield: 4 servings

Nutrition information per serving:

Calories	335
Fat	21 g
Cholesterol	90 mg
Sodium	450 mg
Carbohydrate	20 g
Protein	17 g

One of the most sophisticated cuisines in the Mediterranean region is that of Turkey. Turkish influence was far-reaching during the Ottoman Empire, which ended early in this century, and the court food developed for the sultans' dinners is represented by many recipes still popular today. In Classic Turkish Cooking, Ghillie Basan presents a savory stuffed pasta dish called manti *that is as complex and flavorful as classics from Italy and China.*

½ pound ground lamb
½ onion, finely chopped
1 tablespoon minced fresh parsley
⅛ teaspoon ground red pepper
⅛ teaspoon ground black pepper
⅛ teaspoon ground cumin
⅛ teaspoon dried oregano
⅛ teaspoon dried mint
Pinch of salt
½ cup plain yogurt
3 cloves garlic, crushed with salt
20 wonton or ravioli wrappers
2 cups chicken, beef, or lamb broth
¼ cup (½ stick) unsalted butter, melted
Paprika

1. Heat oven to 350°F. Place lamb, onion, parsley, spices, and dried herbs in a mixing bowl; blend well. Season with salt and black pepper. Set aside. Beat yogurt, garlic, and salt to taste together in a medium bowl; set aside.

2. Lay out wonton or ravioli wrappers on a work surface; roll out thinly. Place a small portion of meat mixture in the center of each square. Bring the four corners up the sides; pinch together. Arrange manti in a single layer in a greased roasting pan. Bake, uncovered, until golden brown, about 20 minutes.

3. Heat broth to a boil in a small saucepan. Remove manti from oven; pour broth over. Cover the pan with foil; return to oven. Bake until manti have absorbed liquid, 15 to 20 minutes. Transfer the baked manti to a serving dish; spoon yogurt sauce over. Top with melted butter; sprinkle with paprika. Serve hot.

Samosas

Preparation time: 30 minutes

Cooking time: 2 to 3 minutes
    per batch

Yield: 8 to 10 pastries

Nutrition information per
samosa (based on 10):

Calories	220
Fat	8 g
Cholesterol	3 mg
Sodium	305 mg
Carbohydrate	33 g
Protein	5 g

Authentic Indian flavor can be captured using a heady mix of readily available spices, as in this Indian turnover recipe from the Chicago Tribune's "Fast Food" column. Preparation is speeded by using prepared egg roll wrappers.

2 tablespoons vegetable oil
1¼ teaspoons whole cumin seeds
½ teaspoon whole coriander seeds
1 hot green chili, minced
1 piece gingerroot, about a ½-inch cube, minced
1 onion, diced
4 red potatoes, cooked and diced
¾ cup peas
½ teaspoon salt
⅓ cup chopped cilantro
8 to 10 egg roll wrappers
Vegetable oil for frying

1. Heat oil in a large skillet over medium-high heat. Add cumin and coriander; cook until fragrant, 2 minutes. Add chili and ginger; cook 1 minute. Reduce heat to medium; add onion. Cook, stirring occasionally, until onion softens, 4 to 5 minutes. Add potatoes, peas, and salt; cook 1 minute. Remove from heat; add cilantro. Filling can be made a day ahead and refrigerated; bring to room temperature before using.

2. Spoon filling onto the bottom half of each egg roll wrapper, using about ⅓ cup filling for each. Fold over, trim into half-moons, and pinch edges closed.

3. Heat several inches of oil to 375°F in a deep saucepan. Fry pastries, several at a time, until they are crisp and golden, 2 to 3 minutes. Drain on paper towels.

Spicy Shrimp Empanadas

These bite-sized turnovers are a favorite of South American cooking. Serve as part of a first course or as an hors d'oeuvre with wine or beer.

2 teaspoons vegetable oil plus more for frying
¼ cup finely chopped onion
1 small hot chili, seeded if desired, chopped
2 teaspoons grated orange zest
¼ teaspoon cumin seed
Salt to taste
⅔ pound peeled shrimp, chopped
⅓ cup unsweetened coconut milk
½ cup cilantro leaves
10 ready-made empanada or egg roll wrappers

Preparation time: 30 minutes
Cooking time: 3 minutes per batch
Yield: 10 empanadas

Nutrition information per empanada:

Calories	120
Fat	7 g
Cholesterol	60 mg
Sodium	115 mg
Carbohydrate	6 g
Protein	7 g

1. Heat 2 teaspoons oil in a skillet. Add onion, chili, orange zest, cumin, and salt. Cook over high heat, stirring often, until onion is soft, 3 to 4 minutes. Add shrimp; cook just until it turns pink, 1 to 2 minutes. Remove from heat. Stir in coconut milk. Transfer mixture to a food processor or blender; add cilantro. Chop coarsely, using on and off turns.

2. Spoon about 3 tablespoons filling slightly off center of each empanada wrapper. Fold over like a turnover. Crimp the edges with the tines of a fork to tightly seal.

3. Heat several inches of oil in a heavy, deep saucepan to 350°F. Fry empanadas in batches so the pan is not crowded, until crisp and golden, 2 to 3 minutes per batch. Drain on paper towels. Serve warm.

Pork Tamales

Preparation time: 1½ hours

Cooking time: 2½ hours

Yield: About 2 dozen tamales

Nutrition information per tamale:

Calories	210
Fat	12 g
Cholesterol	25 mg
Sodium	285 mg
Carbohydrate	17 g
Protein	8 g

NOTE

Masa harina is flour made from dried corn kernels that have been cooked in lime water.

Artist and printmaker Tony Galigo prepares these tamales with his mother for Day of the Dead feasts. For the best-tasting tamales, use the finest mole paste you can find and homemade lard (found in some Hispanic markets) rather than the hydrogenated variety.

3–4 dozen dried corn husks

Pork Filling

1½ pounds lean boneless pork stew meat, cut into
   ½-inch pieces

4 cups water

1 small white onion, chopped

2 cloves garlic, minced

½ teaspoon salt

Mole Sauce

1 8-ounce jar mole paste

½ cup pureed canned or fresh, ripe tomatoes

Salt to taste

Tamale Filling

4 cups masa harina, see Note

1 teaspoon baking soda

1 teaspoon salt

2½ cups water or broth from cooking pork

1 cup homemade lard or vegetable shortening

Chopped cilantro for garnish

1. Soak dried corn husks in several changes of hot water to soften, 1 hour or more. For the pork filling, put pork, water, onion, garlic, and salt into a medium nonreactive saucepan. Simmer gently, partly covered, until pork is fork-tender, about 1½ hours. Strain; reserve meat and broth.

2. For the mole sauce, put mole paste into a medium nonre-active saucepan. Whisk in 2½ cups of the reserved pork broth. Heat to a simmer, whisking constantly until smooth; simmer about 15 minutes. Stir in tomatoes; season with salt.

3. For the tamale filling, combine masa harina, baking soda, and salt in a bowl. Stir in 2½ cups water (or any remaining pork broth) to moisten. Beat lard or shortening in the large bowl of an electric mixer until very light. Gradually beat in masa harina mixture to make a light, fluffy batter.

4. To assemble, lay one corn husk out flat. Spread about ¼ cup masa harina mixture over the center of the husk to a ¼-inch thickness. Place a few pieces of cooked pork and 1 teaspoon mole sauce in the center. Pick up the long sides of the corn husk to completely enclose the filling. Fold up the two short sides. If the husk is small, wrap the whole thing in a second husk. Repeat to use all the masa harina mixture.

5. Line the bottom of a steamer with some of the remaining corn husks. Fill the steamer with tamales, standing them upright. Cover the tamales with a few corn husks. Set the steamer into a pot containing 1 inch of water. Cover tightly; steam over medium heat, checking water level periodically, 45 minutes.

6. To serve, heat the remaining mole sauce. Open up each tamale and pour a bit of the sauce over; sprinkle with cilantro.

Spicy Beef Salpicon

Preparation time: 30 minutes
Cooking time: About 2 hours
Chilling time: 2 hours
Yield: 6 servings

Nutrition information per
serving (without tortillas):

Calories	680
Fat	57 g
Cholesterol	135 mg
Sodium	300 mg
Carbohydrate	6 g
Protein	36 g

This shredded, spicy beef brisket is rolled into warm tortillas with lettuce, tomatoes, and avocados for a typical casual Mexican snack or light meal called salpicon. *Serve it with sangria or margaritas.*

3 pounds beef brisket
1 quart water
1 large onion, quartered
½ teaspoon salt
½ teaspoon freshly ground black pepper
4 plum tomatoes, quartered and sliced
1 large bunch cilantro, chopped
2 to 3 serrano chilies, seeded and minced
¼ cup olive oil
4 to 8 tablespoons distilled white vinegar to taste
Salt to taste
Freshly ground black pepper to taste
½ head iceberg lettuce, rinsed, patted dry, and finely
   shredded
2 ripe avocados, peeled and sliced thin
Canned chipotle chilies, optional
Warm corn tortillas

1. Put beef, water, onion, and ½ teaspoon each salt and black pepper into a 4-quart dutch oven. Heat to a simmer; reduce heat to low. Simmer, tightly covered, until meat is very tender, about 2 hours. Remove meat from liquid; cool. (Freeze broth for another use.)

2. Pull cooled meat into thin shreds. Mix meat with tomatoes, cilantro, serrano chilies, oil, and vinegar to taste. Add salt and black pepper to taste. Cover; chill 2 hours.

3. Let meat come to room temperature. Arrange half of the shredded lettuce on a serving platter. Toss remaining lettuce with meat mixture. Arrange meat mixture over lettuce on serving platter. Garnish with sliced avocados and chipotle chilies. At table, spoon meat, lettuce, avocados, and chilies inside warm tortillas; roll up for eating.

Dilled Roast Beef and Red Cabbage Lefse Wraps

Preparation time: 15 minutes

Yield: 2 servings

Nutrition information per serving:

Calories	230
Fat	11 g
Cholesterol	40 mg
Sodium	235 mg
Carbohydrate	19 g
Protein	15 g

Wrapped sandwiches are a portable, easy snack in many cuisines. Here, we suggest roast beef and cabbage rolled in lefse, a flat bread also known as Scandinavian potato bread or Norwegian wrapping bread, to be served as part of a smorgasbord. Usually round, lefse occasionally is sold in rectangular pieces.

1 teaspoon raspberry or red-wine vinegar
1 teaspoon vegetable oil
1 teaspoon salt
1 teaspoon freshly ground pepper
¾ cup thinly sliced red cabbage
1 tablespoon prepared horseradish cream
2 lefse (Scandinavian potato bread rounds)
1 tablespoon minced fresh dill
2 large Boston lettuce leaves
3 to 4 ounces thinly sliced cooked roast beef

1. Mix together vinegar, oil, salt, and pepper in a medium bowl. Toss in cabbage to coat.

2. Spread horseradish cream over lefse; sprinkle with small amount of dill. Top with lettuce, roast beef, cabbage mixture, and remaining dill. Roll up like a burrito.

Lemon Crab Smorrebrod

A Danish luncheon of the small sandwiches known as smorrebrod (pronounced smeur-breudt) means setting out artfully constructed selections of fish, meat, and vegetables arranged on thinly sliced, buttered rye bread. In an article on the subject, food writer Andrew Schloss suggests serving two or three smorrebrod per person. Because they are open-faced and often precariously stacked, they are eaten with a knife and fork.

3 tablespoons mayonnaise or plain yogurt

2 teaspoons fresh lemon juice

1 clove garlic, minced

Salt to taste

Ground red pepper to taste

12 ounces lump crabmeat, cleaned

3 green onions (white part only), thinly sliced

12 thin slices French bread or 6 small rolls, halved

6 teaspoons unsalted butter, softened

12 thin slices cucumber

12 slices Japanese pickled ginger, optional

12 chives, cut in half lengthwise

1. Mix mayonnaise, lemon juice, garlic, salt, and red pepper together in a medium bowl. Add crabmeat and green onion; toss to mix.

2. Spread each slice of bread with ½ teaspoon butter. Top each with a cucumber slice, a mound of crab mixture, a pickled ginger slice, and two pieces of chives.

Preparation time: 30 minutes

Yield: 6 servings

Nutrition information per serving:

Calories	505
Fat	10 g
Cholesterol	100 mg
Sodium	985 mg
Carbohydrate	56 g
Protein	27 g

VARIATION

For lemon salmon smorrebrod, follow the recipe but substitute 1 14-ounce can salmon for the crab. Clean salmon of skin and bones before adding it to the other ingredients.

Risotto Cakes with Shrimp and Mustard Sauce

Preparation time: 45 minutes

Cooking time: 1 hour

Yield: 8 servings

Glenview, Illinois, cooking teacher Julie Kearney suggests to her students that this recipe is a practical and delicious way to use up leftovers of that northern Italian rice favorite, risotto.

Nutrition information per serving:

Calories	375
Fat	16 g
Cholesterol	75 mg
Sodium	795 mg
Carbohydrate	45 g
Protein	12 g

3 tablespoons olive oil

2 cups rice, Italian arborio preferred

1 medium onion, chopped

1 cup chopped wild mushrooms

4 cloves garlic, minced

7 cups chicken broth, heated

1 large egg

½ cup whipping cream

½ teaspoon sugar

1 to 2 tablespoons Dijon mustard

1½ teaspoons prepared horseradish

2 tablespoons butter

1 tablespoon minced fresh thyme leaves, or 1 teaspoon dried

16 medium shrimp, peeled and deveined

8 sprigs fresh thyme

Chopped tomato for garnish

1. Heat 2 tablespoons oil in a large saucepan over medium heat. Add rice; stir to coat grains. Add onion, mushrooms, and 2 cloves garlic. Cook, stirring, 5 minutes.

2. Add ½ cup hot chicken broth; simmer, stirring, until broth is absorbed, about 5 minutes. Stir in another ½ cup until absorbed. Continue cooking, adding broth by ½-cupfuls, until all broth has been absorbed and rice is creamy but with slight firmness, about 40 minutes total.

3. Cool to room temperature; add egg and shape into 16 patties. Meanwhile, to make the mustard sauce, whip cream until soft peaks form. Stir in sugar, mustard, and horseradish. Chill sauce until ready to serve, up to 1 hour.

4. Heat remaining 1 tablespoon oil and 1 tablespoon butter in a large skillet. Add as many patties as possible without crowding pan. Cook until golden brown, 2 to 4 minutes. Turn and cook for an additional 2 to 4 minutes. Transfer to a warm oven while cooking remaining patties.

5. Clean the skillet, heat the remaining 1 tablespoon butter, and add remaining 2 cloves garlic and the thyme and shrimp. Cook, stirring, only until shrimp turn pink, about 2 minutes.

6. Divide the risotto cakes among 8 warm serving plates. Top each cake with a dollop of mustard sauce and a cooked shrimp. Garnish each plate with a sprig of thyme and a little chopped tomato. Serve at once.

French Country Pâté

Preparation time: 30 minutes

Cooking time: 1½ hours

Chilling time: 24 hours

Yield: 10 appetizer servings

Nutrition information per serving:

Calories	600
Fat	59 g
Cholesterol	165 mg
Sodium	740 mg
Carbohydrate	2 g
Protein	15 g

NOTE

For four-spice mixture (*quatre-épices*), mix together 2 teaspoons freshly ground pepper, preferably white, and ¼ teaspoon each, ground: cloves, ginger, nutmeg. Store in a tightly closed jar. In place of the teaspoon of four-spice mixture, you also can use ½ bay leaf ground with ¾ teaspoon thyme.

This delicious pâté from the late cooking instructor Peter Kump is a chunky pâté, garlicky and hearty, rich with flavor and typically French. Enjoy it at a French-style picnic with a bottle of wine and fresh French bread, some cheeses, and French cornichon pickles.

½ pound ground fresh pork

½ pound ground fresh pork fat

½ pound ground lean veal or beef

½ pound pork liver

1 tablespoon unsalted butter

1 small onion, chopped

1 large egg

2 tablespoons Armagnac, cognac, or other brandy

3 cloves garlic, minced

1 teaspoon four-spice mixture, see Note

1 tablespoon salt

½ teaspoon freshly ground pepper

1 tablespoon flour

10 ounces pork fat to line mold, sliced very thin

¼ pound ham, cut in ¼-inch slices, then cut in ¼-inch strips

1. Mix ground pork, pork fat, and veal together in a large bowl with hands. Puree liver in a food processor fitted with a metal blade or in a blender; add to meat and mix again.

2. Melt butter in a small skillet. Add onion; cook until translucent, about 5 minutes. Add to meat mixture with egg, Armagnac, garlic, spices, salt, and pepper. Sprinkle with flour; mix well. (Cook a spoonful to taste for seasoning.)

3. Line a 6-cup pâté mold or loaf pan with sliced pork fat. Divide meat mixture into quarters; place one of the quarters on the bottom of the mold. Cover meat with ⅓ of the ham strips, leaving space between strips. Repeat layering, ending with meat mixture. Cover with sliced fat.

4. Heat oven to 350°F. Cover the pâté mold; place the mold in a baking pan and set on the oven rack. Add boiling water to the pan to about a 1-inch depth. Cook until fat juices are clear yellow with no rosy traces, 1¼ to 1½ hours. Discard water; cool pâté to room temperature.

5. Weight down (use unopened cans of food); refrigerate at least 24 hours to develop best flavor. Serve at room temperature.

Basil Frittata with Sausage and Pepper Ragu

Preparation time: 50 minutes
Cooking time: 40 minutes
Yield: 6 servings

Nutrition information per serving:

Calories	390
Fat	31 g
Cholesterol	392 mg
Sodium	840 mg
Carbohydrate	8 g
Protein	19 g

Brunch is an ideal format for connecting with the family or entertaining. This frittata recipe, generously flecked with fresh basil and served with a sausage and pepper ragu, came from Betty Gladden of the Garratt Mansion in Alameda, California.

Ragu

4 ounces (½ package) brown-and-serve breakfast sausages

1 tablespoon unsalted butter

1 small onion, diced

1 clove garlic, minced

2 bell peppers, preferably of different colors, cut in 1-inch squares

1 8-ounce can diced tomatoes

¼ cup minced fresh basil

¼ teaspoon sugar

Salt to taste

Freshly ground black pepper to taste

Frittata

10 large eggs

¾ cup sour cream

¾ teaspoon salt

Freshly ground black pepper to taste

2 tablespoons olive oil

½ cup thinly sliced green onions

2 tablespoons minced fresh basil

⅔ cup freshly grated Parmesan cheese

1. For the ragu, cook sausages over medium heat in a large skillet until browned, about 5 minutes. Remove from pan; cut into 1-inch pieces. Set aside. Melt butter in the same pan. Add onion and garlic; cook until softened, 3 minutes.

   Add bell peppers and cook over medium-high heat, stirring often, until almost tender, 5 minutes.

2. Add tomatoes with their liquid, basil, sugar, salt, and black pepper; heat to a boil. Reduce heat; add sausage pieces. Simmer until thickened, 5 minutes. Adjust seasoning. Keep warm.

3. For the frittata, whisk together eggs, sour cream, salt, and pepper; set aside. Heat oil in a 10-inch ovenproof skillet over medium heat. Add green onions and basil. Cook, stirring, just until onions soften, 1 minute. Add egg mixture; cook until eggs begin to set at edges. Lift the cooked edges using a spatula; tilt the pan slightly so uncooked eggs from the center flow to the edge. Continue to cook until the eggs are just softly set in the center, 5 to 6 minutes.

4. Heat broiler; sprinkle cheese over top of frittata. Broil just until eggs are set, 1 to 2 minutes. Cut into wedges; serve topped with ragu.

Grilled Portobello Panini

Preparation time: 20 minutes
Cooking time: 5 to 7 minutes
Yield: 4 servings

Gina Passantino, of Arlington, Virginia, submitted this Italian sandwich recipe to the Chicago Tribune's "You're the Cook" *column. Portobellos are thick, meaty mushrooms that grill beautifully.*

Nutrition information per serving:

Calories	355
Fat	20 g
Cholesterol	15 mg
Sodium	350 mg
Carbohydrate	34 g
Protein	11 g

¼ cup extra-virgin olive oil plus extra
2 tablespoons chopped fresh basil
2 cloves garlic, minced
Salt to taste
Freshly ground pepper to taste
4 portobello mushroom caps, sliced at an angle into
    4 pieces each
4 kaiser or hard rolls, split
1 large tomato, cut into 4 slices
½ cup shredded Asiago cheese

1. Prepare grill or broiler. Combine olive oil, basil, garlic, salt, and pepper in a small bowl; mix well. Set aside.

2. Brush mushrooms with additional olive oil. Grill or broil, rounded side up, 2 to 3 minutes. Turn mushrooms. Add rolls to grill or broiler. Grill or broil 1 to 2 minutes.

3. Spread a little basil oil mixture on the bottom half of each roll. Top each with a tomato slice, additional basil oil, cheese, mushroom slices, and top of roll. Cut in half to serve.

Ceviche

One of the great dishes of Latin cooking is ceviche, in which the freshest seafoods are marinated in oil and various seasonings and "cooked" with the acid of citrus juice. This recipe comes from the Mexican restaurant Alicia's, located on the Near Northwest Side of Chicago.

Juice of 5 limes
½ pound fillet of boneless whitefish, such as orange roughy, cut into ½-inch dice
½ pound crabmeat, cleaned of cartilage
½ pound medium shrimp, peeled, deveined, and cut into ½-inch dice
2 to 3 jalapeño chilies, seeded and finely diced, optional
2 medium tomatoes, seeded and diced
½ onion, peeled and finely diced
2 tablespoons chopped celery
2 tablespoons chopped cilantro
½ teaspoon dried oregano
1 teaspoon olive oil
1 teaspoon salt
1 ripe avocado, peeled and thinly sliced

1. Pour lime juice into a glass or other nonreactive bowl. Add diced fish, crabmeat, and shrimp. Stir gently to combine seafood and liquid. Refrigerate, stirring occasionally, about 4 hours, or until seafood is opaque and "cooked." (The seafood in this recipe is not cooked over heat.)

2. Add diced chilies, tomatoes, onion, celery, cilantro, oregano, olive oil, and salt to seafood and liquid. Mix gently. If desired, refrigerate to allow flavors to meld from 30 minutes to 4 hours. Transfer ceviche to a platter; garnish with avocado slices.

Preparation time: 30 minutes
Marinating time: 4 hours
Yield: 6 appetizer servings

Nutrition information per serving:

Calories	130
Fat	2 g
Cholesterol	90 mg
Sodium	605 mg
Carbohydrate	4 g
Protein	22 g

Mussels in White Wine Sauce

Preparation time: 35 minutes
Cooking time: 25 minutes
Yield: 8 servings

Nutrition information per serving:

Calories	170
Fat	10 g
Cholesterol	55 mg
Sodium	345 mg
Carbohydrate	7 g
Protein	14 g

Bowls of mussels in white wine are typically found in French brasseries and make a wonderful first course or light meal. The following is adapted from a recipe by chef Jean Joho, who serves this dish at his Brasserie Jo in Chicago's River North neighborhood. Serve this with crusty French bread for dipping into the bowl.

1 tablespoon butter
4 large shallots, minced
1 clove garlic, minced
4 pounds fresh mussels, debearded and well scrubbed
1 cup Alsatian Pinot blanc or other dry white wine
½ cup whipping cream
½ cup minced fresh parsley
Fresh lemon juice to taste
Salt to taste
Freshly ground pepper to taste

1. Melt butter in a large dutch oven. Add shallots and garlic; cook over medium heat until tender, about 3 minutes. Add cleaned mussels and wine. Cover tightly. Steam, shaking pan occasionally, until mussels open, 5 to 7 minutes. Discard any unopened mussels.

2. Transfer mussels to a serving bowl using a slotted spoon; cover and keep warm. Strain cooking liquid through a fine wire mesh strainer or double thickness of cheesecloth into a medium saucepan. Boil over medium-high heat until reduced slightly. Whisk in cream; boil to reduce again until slightly thickened. Stir in parsley, lemon juice, salt, and pepper. Pour over mussels.

Mussels with Lemongrass

In this recipe, inspired by one in the cookbook The Best of
Thailand, *Thai-style mussels are steamed with garlic,
lemongrass, and basil. Red chilies add heat. Look for Thai basil
(also called holy basil) and lemongrass in Thai or Asian food
markets.*

Preparation time: 20 minutes
Cooking time: 5 minutes
Yield: 4 servings

2½ pounds fresh mussels, debearded and well scrubbed
1 13¾-ounce can chicken broth
4 stalks lemongrass, trimmed and cut in 2-inch pieces
8 shallots, thinly sliced
½ cup fresh Thai basil leaves, shredded
Zest of 2 limes
3 cloves garlic, minced
2 small fresh red chilies, seeded
2 small fresh green chilies, seeded
½ teaspoon salt
½ teaspoon sugar
2 tablespoons chopped cilantro

Nutrition information per
serving:

Calories	150
Fat	4 g
Cholesterol	40 mg
Sodium	1,000 mg
Carbohydrate	12 g
Protein	18 g

1. Wash mussels in several changes of cold water. Discard
   any that remain open. Drain well.

2. Pour broth into a 2½-quart saucepan. Add lemongrass,
   shallots, basil, lime zest, garlic, chilies, salt, sugar; heat to
   a simmer. Simmer 5 minutes.

3. Add mussels; toss to coat. Cover; heat to a boil. Cook just
   until all shells are open, 4 to 5 minutes. Discard any closed
   mussels. Divide mussels and broth into four soup bowls.
   Sprinkle each with cilantro.

Soups

Alicia's Restaurant, Milwaukee Avenue

Japanese Udon Soup

Preparation time: 25 minutes

Soaking time: 30 minutes

Cooking time: 30 minutes

Yield: 6 servings

Nutrition information per serving:

Calories	185
Fat	1 g
Cholesterol	0 mg
Sodium	1,895 mg
Carbohydrate	39 g
Protein	6 g

VARIATIONS

Try substituting 1 cup sliced button mushrooms and adding any of the following: sautéed shrimp; cubed, extrafirm tofu (bean curd); or cooked lump crabmeat.

"Bowl cuisine"—a meal in a bowl—embraces many ethnic trends. For time-crunched cooks, it offers the added element of convenience. This Japanese udon soup, from M Cafe, the restaurant in Chicago's Museum of Contemporary Art, is both filling and low-fat. Dashi, one of the major ingredients, is a soup stock of dried bonito tuna flakes, dried kelp, and water. Dashi powder and other Japanese ingredients are sold at Asian markets, but also may be found in health-food stores and some supermarkets.

8 to 10 dried shiitake mushrooms, soaked ½ hour in boiling water and drained

¼ cup dashi powder (Japanese fish stock base)

3 tablespoons soy sauce

1½ teaspoons mirin (rice wine)

1 10- to 12-ounce package Japanese udon noodles

½ napa cabbage, shredded

1 bunch green onions, trimmed and sliced

¼ pound fresh snow peas, julienned

¼ pound fresh bean sprouts

Seven-spice chili pepper (*shichimi-togarashi*), optional

1. Trim off mushroom stems; discard. Slice caps thinly. Heat 2 quarts water with the mushrooms, dashi powder, soy sauce, and mirin to a boil in a large saucepan over medium heat. Reduce heat to low; simmer 20 minutes.

2. Heat 2 quarts salted water to a boil in a large pot. Add noodles. Cook until just al dente, about 8 to 10 minutes. Drain; rinse.

3. Combine cabbage, onions, snow peas, and bean sprouts in a large bowl. Divide cabbage mixture among 6 large bowls. Ladle noodles and broth into bowls. Serve with a dash of seven-spice chili pepper, if desired.

Caramelized Fennel Soup

The highly touted Mediterranean diet, says Patricia Wells, a food writer based in France, is somewhat idealized. Her neighbors in Provence, for example, still eat a high-fat diet. And yet, the region's fresh, local produce provides a starting point for a variety of distinctive dishes, including this luscious fennel soup. Fennel is generally available from fall to spring; buy crisp bulbs with fresh-looking greenery and no brown spots. This recipe was adapted from Patricia Wells at Home in Provence.

6 tablespoons extra-virgin olive oil
2 pounds fennel bulbs, trimmed and minced, see Note
Bouquet garni: 1 sprig each fresh rosemary, parsley, and
    thyme, plus one bay leaf, tied with twine
4 cups homemade or canned vegetable or chicken broth
½ cup whipping cream, optional
Sea salt to taste

1. Heat oil in a large, heavy-bottomed saucepan. Add fennel, stirring to coat with oil. Cover; cook over low heat 10 minutes, stirring occasionally. Do not burn. Remove lid; continue to cook over low heat. The fennel pieces should gradually brown and caramelize. Add bouquet garni and broth; simmer, covered, 30 minutes.

2. Discard bouquet garni. Puree soup in batches in a food processor; return to the pan. The soup should be creamy but not totally smooth. Stir in cream, if using, and salt; reheat. Taste for seasoning.

Preparation time: 30 minutes
Cooking time: 45 minutes
Yield: 4 servings

Nutrition information per serving:

Calories	390
Fat	33 g
Cholesterol	40 mg
Sodium	905 mg
Carbohydrate	18 g
Protein	8 g

NOTE
Fennel has a tough outer skin. It's well worth peeling with a vegetable peeler.

Gazpacho

Preparation time: 30 minutes

Chilling time: Several hours

Yield: 12 1-cup servings

Gazpacho is a cold soup from Spain. It doesn't need cooking, making it an ideal summertime entree. A variety of vegetables can be used in gazpacho; this recipe, developed in the Chicago Tribune *Test Kitchen, puts fennel in a starring role. If fennel isn't available, celery may be substituted.*

Nutrition information per serving:

Calories	70
Fat	3 g
Cholesterol	0 mg
Sodium	430 mg
Carbohydrate	12 g
Protein	2 g

1 cucumber, unpeeled and seeded
1 large red bell pepper
1 large green bell pepper
1 large fennel bulb, trimmed
3 large tomatoes, seeded
3 small red knob onions
1 clove garlic
1 48-ounce can tomato vegetable juice (such as V-8)
8 oil-packed sun-dried tomatoes, minced
2 tablespoons balsamic vinegar
2 tablespoons olive oil
Crushed red pepper flakes to taste
Chopped fresh basil to taste
Salt to taste

1. Finely chop all vegetables except sun-dried tomatoes by hand or in a food processor. (If using a food processor, chop in small batches using on/off turns so they are not too fine.)

2. Place vegetables in a large bowl. Add tomato juice, sun-dried tomatoes, vinegar, oil, pepper flakes, basil, and salt. Chill well before serving. Adjust seasoning before serving.

Satay with Creamy Peanut Dipping Sauce, page 10

Pork Tamales, page 26

Basil Frittata with Sausage and Pepper Ragu, page 36

Pasta Salad with Tomato Compote, page 79

Coconut Shrimp Curry with Peas, page 89

Mediterranean Chicken with Cucumber Sauce and Couscous, page 102

Spicy Orange Beef, page 116

Thai-Style Hamburgers, page 119

Ukrainian Meatless Borscht

The neighborhood known as Ukrainian Village in Chicago is home to about 8,000 people of Ukrainian extraction, as well as many from other Eastern European countries. Angelina Pleskanka, from St. Nicholas Cathedral Parish School, offered this basic Ukrainian borscht, a hearty beet soup. A variety of other ingredients can be added to this soup, Pleskanka said, but the secret of a good borscht is simple: "It's love." This version is meatless and very low in calories. Serve it hot or cold.

4 to 5 fresh beets, trimmed
9 cups water
2 medium onions, diced
2 carrots, peeled and cut in thin strips
3 ribs celery, diced
2 medium leeks, trimmed and minced
1 clove garlic, crushed
2 bay leaves
2 cups spicy tomato vegetable juice (such as V-8)
1 tablespoon salt or to taste
Freshly ground pepper to taste
¼ cup minced fresh dill
Whipping cream or sour cream, optional

1. Cook beets in water to cover in a medium saucepan until tender, about 40 minutes; drain. Cool. Peel; cut into thin strips.

2. Put 9 cups water and the onions, carrots, celery, leeks, garlic, and bay leaves into a large soup pot. Heat to a boil; simmer until vegetables are tender, about 20 minutes.

3. Add cooked beets and tomato juice. Heat to a boil; simmer about 10 minutes. Season with salt and pepper. Remove bay leaves. Add dill just before serving. Serve in bowls with a dollop of whipping cream or sour cream, if desired.

Preparation time: 40 minutes
Cooking time: 40 minutes
Yield: 12 servings

Nutrition information per serving (without cream):

Calories	35
Fat	0 g
Cholesterol	0 mg
Sodium	720 mg
Carbohydrate	9 g
Protein	1 g

Polish Cream of Mushroom Soup

Soaking time: 1 hour or more
Preparation time: 25 minutes
Cooking time: 1½ hours
Yield: 8 servings

Nutrition information per serving:

Calories	165
Fat	12 g
Cholesterol	25 mg
Sodium	345 mg
Carbohydrate	12 g
Protein	4 g

Polish-American Marala Ciesla shared her recipe for this rich, earthy-tasting soup made with dried mushrooms she brought back from visits to Poland. Imported dried mushrooms are sold at Polish food stores and delicatessens and some supermarkets.

7 large dried mushrooms, about ½ ounce, preferably cèpes or porcini
8 cups water
2 carrots, peeled and cut in 1-inch pieces
2 ribs celery, cut in 1-inch pieces
2 sprigs parsley
1 medium onion, unpeeled and halved
1 teaspoon salt
4 peppercorns
1 bay leaf
1 pound fresh mushrooms, sliced
2 cups sour cream
3 tablespoons flour
Buttered croutons

1. Rinse dried mushrooms and soak in 2 cups water at least 1 hour. Put remaining 6 cups water and the carrots, celery, parsley, onion, salt, peppercorns, and bay leaf in a large saucepan. Simmer gently over medium heat, 1 hour. Strain; discard vegetables.

2. Combine fresh mushrooms with soaked mushrooms and soaking water in a separate saucepan. Cover; simmer 20 minutes. Transfer to a blender or food processor fitted with a metal blade; puree.

3. Blend sour cream and flour together in a small bowl. Add to blender; mix until smooth. Add mixture in blender to strained stock; simmer 3 to 4 minutes, without letting soup come to a boil. Serve with buttered croutons.

Garlic Soup

Yes, this French soup developed by Chicago Tribune *food and wine columnist William Rice is loaded with garlic—but it also has a sweet, rich flavor. Long a favorite in Europe, garlic has slowly emerged as an essential ingredient in American cooking. A member of the lily family, garlic has many medicinal benefits. It's also inexpensive and keeps for up to eight weeks when stored in a cool, dry spot.*

2 heads fresh garlic, unpeeled and separated into cloves
4 cups chicken broth
1 medium onion, chopped
2 carrots, peeled and chopped
3 small red potatoes, peeled and chopped
2 ribs celery, chopped
½ teaspoon dried basil
1 tablespoon chopped fresh parsley
Salt to taste
Pepper to taste

1. Cover garlic cloves with 2 cups water in a saucepan; heat to a boil. Simmer 5 minutes. Drain; let cool. Remove skins.

2. Return garlic to pan. Add chicken broth, onion, carrots, potatoes, celery, basil, and 2 teaspoons parsley. Heat to a boil; reduce heat to a simmer. Cover; cook until vegetables are very soft, 30 to 35 minutes. Let cool slightly.

3. Puree soup in a blender or food processor; season with salt and pepper. (Soup may be done ahead to this point.) Return soup to a clean pan; heat. If it seems too thick, add broth or water. Adjust seasoning. Sprinkle with remaining 1 teaspoon parsley.

Preparation time: 25 minutes
Cooking time: 40 minutes
Yield: 4 servings

Nutrition information per serving:

Calories	130
Fat	2 g
Cholesterol	0 mg
Sodium	810 mg
Carbohydrate	21 g
Protein	8 g

Split Pea Soup with Cardamom-Saffron Rice Cakes

Soaking time: 2 hours
Preparation time: 50 minutes
Cooking time: 1 to 1½ hours
Yield: 6 servings

Nutrition information per serving:

Calories	310
Fat	3 g
Cholesterol	0 mg
Sodium	30 mg
Carbohydrate	59 g
Protein	10 g

A variety of seeds can be found in the dishes of India; one of the hottest is mustard seed, which plays a prominent role in this Indian soup recipe adapted from Yamuna's Table, *by Yamuna Devi. Mustard seed has an earthier, nuttier flavor than prepared mustard, notes the Chicago Tribune's "Good Eating" section staff writer Kristin Eddy in a story on hot spices. When using mustard seeds for cooking, crush or toast the seeds to release their intense flavor.*

Soup
¾ cup yellow split peas, soaked in water 2 hours and drained
2 tablespoons long-grain rice
7 cups water or chicken broth
1 tablespoon grated gingerroot
1 to 2 jalapeño chilies, seeded and minced
½ teaspoon ground turmeric
2 cups chopped cauliflower
Salt to taste
Ground black pepper to taste

Rice Cakes
5 cups water
1½ cups long-grain rice, preferably basmati
2 bay leaves
1 stick cinnamon
Salt to taste
Nonstick olive oil spray
½ teaspoon cardamom seeds, crushed
Large pinch saffron threads

Toasted Spice Oil
1 teaspoon mustard seeds
1 teaspoon cumin seeds

1 tablespoon nut, seed, or vegetable oil

3 tablespoons chopped fresh cilantro, mint, basil, or
   parsley for garnish

1. For the soup, combine split peas, rice, 7 cups water, ginger, chilies, turmeric, and cauliflower in a large, heavy-
   bottomed pot. Heat to a boil; partly cover and reduce heat
   to low. Simmer until split peas fall apart, 1 to 1½ hours.
   Cool slightly; puree in batches in a food processor fitted
   with a metal blade or in a blender. Return to pot. Season
   with salt and pepper; gently heat.

2. For the rice cakes, heat oven to 450°F. Heat 5 cups water
   to a boil in a large saucepan over high heat. Stir in rice,
   bay leaves, cinnamon stick, and salt. Cook 10 minutes.
   Transfer to a strainer; rinse under cold water. Discard cinnamon stick and bay leaves. Generously spray six 3- to 4-
   inch ovenproof custard cups or molds with olive oil.
   Sprinkle cardamom seeds and saffron threads in the pans.
   Distribute rice evenly among the pans and pack firmly.
   Spray with olive oil. Bake 12 minutes. Carefully unmold.

3. For spice oil, toast mustard seeds in a small skillet over
   medium heat, covered, until seeds pop and crackle. Add
   cumin seeds and oil; cook about 5 seconds. Swirl toasted
   spice oil into soup. Divide soup among bowls. Place a rice
   cake in the center of each; garnish with chopped cilantro.

Red Lentil Soup with Chicken

Preparation time: 25 minutes

Cooking time: 2 hours

Yield: 5 servings

Nutrition information per serving:

Calories	395
Fat	10 g
Cholesterol	35 mg
Sodium	1,195 mg
Carbohydrate	50 g
Protein	29 g

NOTE

Harissa, a fiery sauce from Tunisia made with hot chili peppers, garlic, cumin, and other spices, lends some heat. It is sold in cans and bottles in some supermarkets and Middle Eastern food markets.

In The Whole World Loves Chicken Soup, *author Mimi Sheraton celebrates the culinary comfort-zone-in-a-bowl. This red lentil soup gets flavor from a rich stock and several spices such as saffron and ginger.*

1 chicken, 3½ to 4 pounds, quartered

10 cups water, or more

2 tablespoons olive oil or unsalted butter

2 ribs celery, diced

1 medium carrot, chopped

1 medium onion, chopped

1½ cups red lentils, rinsed twice in cold water

½ cup crushed tomatoes

1 clove garlic

Large pinch ground saffron

Large pinch ground ginger

⅛ teaspoon harissa, see Note, or ¼ to ½ teaspoon crushed red pepper flakes

Salt to taste, about 2½ teaspoons

1 cup vermicelli, broken into 1½-inch lengths

Chopped cilantro for garnish

Lemon wedges for garnish

1. Put chicken and giblets (except liver) in a 4- to 5-quart pot; add water to cover. Heat to a boil; reduce to a simmer. Skim off any foam. Partly cover; simmer while preparing vegetables.

2. Heat oil in a small skillet. Cook celery, carrot, and onion until soft, about 7 minutes. Add to soup along with lentils, tomatoes, garlic, saffron, ginger, harissa, and salt.

3. Cover; simmer gently until chicken is falling from bones and lentils are disintegrating, 1 to 1½ hours. Stir frequently to prevent scorching, adding more water as needed.

4. Remove chicken; cool. Remove meat from skin and bones. Dice or shred meat and return to soup. Add vermicelli; cook 15 minutes. Adjust seasonings. Pour into bowls; garnish with cilantro and lemon wedges.

Chicken, Escarole, and White Bean Soup

Preparation time: 40 minutes

Chilling time: Overnight

Cooking time: 3 hours,
   25 minutes

Yield: 8 servings

Nutrition information per serving:

Calories	210
Fat	11 g
Cholesterol	15 mg
Sodium	150 mg
Carbohydrate	20 g
Protein	10 g

Tried-and-true chicken soup assumes an Italian flair in this version from chef Paul Bartolotta of Spiaggia restaurant on Chicago's Michigan Avenue. This soup's robust flavor starts with the from-scratch stock. "There's no question that stock is the foundation of a lot of great cooking," Bartolotta told the Chicago Tribune. *His surprise flavor enhancer for stock is a Parmigiano-Reggiano cheese rind.*

Stock

½ large onion, unpeeled

2 whole cloves

6 pounds mixed chicken legs, thighs, and wings

1 gallon water

2 bay leaves

2 garlic cloves, peeled

1 celery rib

1 carrot

1 piece Parmigiano-Reggiano rind, up to 6 ounces

1½ teaspoons salt

½ teaspoon whole black peppercorns

Soup

¼ cup (½ stick) unsalted butter

2 tablespoons extra-virgin olive oil

1 onion, diced

1 carrot, diced

1 celery rib, diced

1 medium head escarole, coarsely chopped

1 cup cooked or canned small white beans or cannelini beans

½ teaspoon salt

Extra-virgin olive oil to taste

Freshly ground black pepper to taste

1. For stock, put onion, cut side down, into a foil-lined cast-iron skillet. Cook over medium-high heat, watching closely, until onion caramelizes and browns on bottom, about 10 minutes. Pierce onion with two cloves; transfer to a large stockpot.

2. Cut chickens into pieces. Add chicken pieces, water, bay leaves, garlic, celery, carrot, cheese rind, salt, and peppercorns. Heat to a slow boil, skimming the surface occasionally. Reduce heat and simmer gently, skimming top periodically, about 3 hours. Add water to keep chicken covered if necessary.

3. Remove chicken pieces from broth. When cool enough to handle, remove meat from skin and bones. Wrap meat and refrigerate. Strain broth; refrigerate overnight so fat solidifies. Remove and discard fat.

4. For soup, heat butter and oil in a large saucepan over medium heat. Add onion, carrot, and celery; cook gently, stirring occasionally, until vegetables are tender, 12 to 15 minutes. Do not let brown.

5. Add escarole; cook and stir just until wilted. Add 6 cups stock (freeze remaining stock for other uses), beans, salt, and reserved chicken meat; simmer so flavors blend, about 10 minutes. Ladle into bowls. Drizzle olive oil over each serving. Sprinkle generously with freshly ground pepper.

Chili Black Bean Soup

Preparation time: 10 minutes
Cooking time: 5 minutes
Yield: 3 servings

Nutrition information per serving:

Calories	170
Fat	1 g
Cholesterol	0 mg
Sodium	1,035 mg
Carbohydrate	33 g
Protein	10 g

This quick-to-make Mexican soup developed in the Chicago Tribune *Test Kitchen takes advantage of canned black beans and Mexican-style stewed tomatoes. A teaspoon of adobo sauce from canned chipotles adds a smoky kick. Look for the canned chipotles in the Mexican food aisle of supermarkets or specialty stores.*

1 15-ounce can black beans, undrained
1 14½-ounce can stewed tomatoes, Mexican-style preferred
½ cup beef broth
1 teaspoon sauce from canned chipotles in adobo sauce or hot sauce to taste
½ teaspoon chili powder
¼ teaspoon ground cumin
Plain yogurt, optional

1. Reserve ⅓ cup beans. Put remaining beans with their liquid in a blender or a food processor fitted with a metal blade. Puree until smooth. Add about ¾ of the tomatoes; process until tomatoes are coarsely chopped.

2. Put bean-tomato mixture and reserved beans into a medium saucepan. Stir in broth, adobo sauce, chili powder, and cumin. Heat until hot. Chop remaining tomatoes. Serve soup in mugs; top each with a spoonful of chopped tomatoes and plain yogurt, if desired.

Basque Sausage and Potato Soup

A sturdy soup doesn't have to take hours to prepare. Spanish-style chorizo or andouille sausage gives this Basque soup a robust flavor.

½ pound smoked spicy sausage, preferably Spanish-style
   chorizo or andouille, cut into ½-inch slices
1 large onion, diced
2 ribs celery, diced
1 large red potato, cut in 1-inch chunks
2 plum tomatoes, diced
3 cups reduced-sodium chicken broth
1 sprig fresh thyme or 1 teaspoon dried thyme
1 to 2 teaspoons sherry vinegar
Salt to taste
Freshly ground pepper to taste

1. Combine sausage and onion in a large pot. Cook over medium-high heat, stirring often, until onion is browned, 5 minutes. Stir in celery and potato; cook 1 to 2 minutes.

2. Add tomatoes, chicken broth, and thyme; heat to a boil. Cover; reduce heat to low. Simmer until potatoes are tender, 12 to 15 minutes. Add vinegar, salt, and pepper to taste.

Preparation time: 15 minutes
Cooking time: 25 minutes
Yield: 4 servings

Nutrition information per serving:

Calories	300
Fat	22 g
Cholesterol	50 mg
Sodium	1,140 mg
Carbohydrate	9 g
Protein	17 g

Alicia's Seven Seas Soup

Preparation time: 40 minutes
Cooking time: 25 minutes
Yield: 4 servings

This elaborate Mexican soup, with six kinds of fish and shellfish, comes from Maria Villanueva, owner of Alicia's Restaurant on the Near Northwest Side of Chicago. Dark red, dried guajillo chilies are sold in the Hispanic food section of most large supermarkets and are readily available in Hispanic markets.

Nutrition information per serving:

Calories	485
Fat	15 g
Cholesterol	270 mg
Sodium	1,455 mg
Carbohydrate	14 g
Protein	70 g

2 tablespoons vegetable oil

1 carrot, diced

1 red potato, diced

1 celery rib, diced

1 tomato, diced

1 dried guajillo chili pepper, stemmed, seeded, and finely chopped, or 1 teaspoon crushed red pepper flakes

1 large clove garlic, minced

1 teaspoon ground cumin

1 teaspoon freshly ground black pepper

2 bay leaves

4 cups water

2 tablespoons chopped cilantro

1 teaspoon salt, or to taste

6 fresh clams in the shell

1½ pounds cleaned octopus or cleaned squid, rinsed

½ pound boneless fish fillets, such as orange roughy or cod

½ pound medium shrimp in the shell

1 or 2 lobster tails, optional

1 or 2 king crab legs, optional

1 lime, cut into wedges

Warmed corn tortillas, optional

1. Heat oil in a 4-quart dutch oven or soup pot. Add carrot, potato, celery, and tomato. Cook, stirring, until vegetables are tender, 2 to 3 minutes. Add guajillo chili, garlic, cumin, black pepper, and bay leaves. Cook 1 minute. Add water, 1 tablespoon cilantro, and salt. Heat to a boil. Reduce heat; let simmer while preparing seafood.

2. Scrub clams very well under running water. Cut octopus into ½-inch dice, if using. Cut squid bodies into ¼-inch-wide rings and cut tentacles into bite-sized pieces, if using. Cut fish fillets crosswise into 2-inch pieces.

3. Add clams, octopus or squid, fish fillet pieces, shrimp, and optional lobster tails and crab legs to soup. Heat to a boil. Reduce heat to a simmer; cook, covered, until seafood is tender, 7 to 12 minutes.

4. Remove lobster tails and crab legs; divide into portions. Place in 4 warm soup bowls; ladle remaining seafood and broth into bowls. Sprinkle with remaining 1 tablespoon cilantro. Pass lime wedges and tortillas at table.

Salmon Soup

Preparation time: 25 minutes

Cooking time: 10 minutes

Yield: 6 servings

Nutrition information per serving:

Calories	215
Fat	11 g
Cholesterol	55 mg
Sodium	80 mg
Carbohydrate	10 g
Protein	19 g

Beatrice Ojakangas, whose grandparents emigrated from Finland to Minnesota, made her own journey back to their homeland in 1958. Ojakangas spoke Finnish and took advantage of the opportunity: "What I really wanted to do was find out about . . . Finnish food. And I did. They wrote down recipes for me on the backs of napkins, scraps of paper, recipes that had probably never been written down before." This salmon soup is included in Ojakangas's cookbook, Scandinavian Feasts. Although fresh salmon fillets are called for, you can use any salmon that is leftover from another meal. Just be sure you don't overcook it. In a pinch, you can even use canned salmon.

2 tablespoons butter

1 large onion, finely chopped

1 small leek, washed and finely sliced

1 rib celery, finely sliced

2 tablespoons flour

3 cups water

1½ tablespoons lemon juice

12 ounces fresh salmon fillets, or cooked or smoked salmon

2 cups whole milk or half-and-half

¼ teaspoon freshly grated nutmeg

½ teaspoon ground ginger

Salt to taste

White pepper to taste

⅓ cup whipping cream or half-and-half, optional

½ cup chopped fresh dill or 6 teaspoons dried dill weed

1. Melt butter in a heavy 4-quart saucepan. Add onion, leek, and celery, and cook over medium heat 2 minutes, stirring constantly. Sprinkle with flour; cook, stirring, 1 minute. Stir in water and lemon juice; simmer, stirring, until lightly thickened.

2. Cut fish into thin slices if it is uncooked. Flake cooked or smoked fish. Add fish and milk to pan; heat through but do not boil. Add nutmeg, ginger, salt, and white pepper. Stir in cream, if using. Ladle soup into soup plates; sprinkle with fresh or dried dill.

Salads

Village Grocery, Chicago Avenue

Mixed Greens with Orange-Cumin Vinaigrette

Preparation time: 15 minutes

Yield: About 4 servings

Nutrition information per serving (using all dressing):

Calories	185
Fat	17 g
Cholesterol	0 mg
Sodium	20 mg
Carbohydrate	4 g
Protein	1 g

Monique King, chef at Soul Kitchen restaurant in Chicago's trendy Wicker Park area, prepares dishes that showcase a melting pot of flavors, particularly Creole, Southwestern, and Caribbean. Here, a tossed salad gets dressed up with a Caribbean vinaigrette. It's quick to make, and versatile too: it also can be used as a marinade.

½ shallot, minced

½ teaspoon ground cumin

Grated zest of ½ orange

Salt to taste

Freshly ground pepper to taste

2 tablespoons fresh orange juice

2 tablespoons sherry vinegar

⅓ cup olive oil

12 ounces (about 4 cups) mixed salad greens

1. Combine shallot, cumin, orange rind, salt, and pepper in a small bowl. Mix well. Stir in orange juice and vinegar. Whisk in oil in a slow stream.

2. Pour about half of the dressing over mixed greens in a serving bowl. Toss well. Add more dressing if needed.

Greek Easter Salad

Easter, the most important of Greek Orthodox religious holidays, heralds a time of devotion, family, tradition, and celebration, in which food plays a central role. This traditional salad, from Papagus Greek Taverna in Chicago's River North neighborhood, gives romaine lettuce a flavor boost with green onions, lemon, and fresh dill.

Preparation time: 25 minutes

Yield: 6 servings

Nutrition information per serving:

Calories	110
Fat	9 g
Cholesterol	0 mg
Sodium	15 mg
Carbohydrate	5 g
Protein	3 g

2 small heads romaine lettuce, rinsed and dried
6 green onions, with some green portion
⅓ cup coarsely chopped fresh dill
⅓ cup coarsely chopped flat-leaf parsley
Juice of ½ small lemon
1½ teaspoons grated or shredded lemon zest
Salt to taste
Freshly ground black pepper to taste
¼ cup extra-virgin olive oil

1. Tear lettuce into bite-sized pieces. Cut green onions lengthwise into quarters, then crosswise into 1-inch pieces.

2. Place romaine, green onions, dill, and parsley into a large bowl. Combine lemon juice, zest, salt, and pepper in a small bowl; slowly whisk in olive oil. Pour over salad; toss to combine. Adjust seasoning to taste with lemon juice, salt, and pepper.

Green Salad with Pesto Dressing and Pine Nuts

Preparation time: 10 minutes

Yield: 4 servings

Nutrition information per serving:

Calories	215
Fat	21 g
Cholesterol	8 mg
Sodium	135 mg
Carbohydrate	4 g
Protein	5 g

This Italian-style salad features a dressing made from pesto, the classic sauce from Genoa made with basil, garlic, pine nuts, Parmesan cheese, and olive oil. But this recipe, developed for a Chicago Tribune "Fast Food" column, speeds up the process by using commercial pesto. Crumbled goat cheese and toasted pine nuts are added at the end for a distinctive finale.

2 tablespoons prepared pesto

1 tablespoon plus 1½ teaspoons seasoned rice vinegar

½ teaspoon Dijon mustard

Salt to taste

Freshly ground pepper to taste

¼ cup olive oil

12 ounces (about 4 cups) mixed salad greens

3 tablespoons crumbled goat cheese

3 tablespoons toasted pine nuts

1. For the dressing, combine pesto, vinegar, mustard, salt, and pepper in a small bowl. Add oil; mix thoroughly.

2. Toss greens with dressing. Divide among 4 plates; top each with cheese, pine nuts, and additional pepper.

Okra Salad

Japanese cuisine prizes aesthetics as well as flavor. "My mother told me to always count the number of colors in a meal, because it's very important to have many different colors," said Miho Tanaka, a native of Japan who gave us this recipe in 1996. "She and my teacher said I should make sure at least thirty ingredients are used each day." Tanaka's fresh okra salad is part of that palette.

6 ounces okra, all about the same size
1 tablespoon sugar
2 teaspoons water
2 teaspoons minced garlic
1 teaspoon soy sauce
1 teaspoon minced green onion
1 teaspoon vegetable oil
½ teaspoon salt

1. Cook okra in a pan of boiling water until it just begins to soften, 4 to 5 minutes. Drain well.

2. Mix remaining ingredients; pour over okra. Toss lightly. Serve at room temperature.

Preparation time: 10 minutes
Cooking time: 5 minutes
Yield: 4 servings

Nutrition information per serving:

Calories	40
Fat	1 g
Cholesterol	0 mg
Sodium	355 mg
Carbohydrate	7 g
Protein	1 g

Orange and Avocado Salad with Chili Lime Dressing

Preparation time: 15 minutes

Yield: 4 servings

When can a salad be cold and hot at the same time? This Mexican-influenced salad starts with the cool flavors of navel oranges and avocado, then gets its heat from jalapeño pepper and chili powder. From a Chicago Tribune "Fast Food" column, this dish also is quick to make.

Nutrition information per serving:

Calories	165
Fat	11 g
Cholesterol	0 mg
Sodium	25 mg
Carbohydrate	18 g
Protein	2 g

4 large leaves red lettuce
3 navel oranges, peeled and cut crosswise into thin slices
½ small red onion, sliced into thin rings
1 ripe avocado, peeled, pitted, and sliced
1 tablespoon lime juice
1 tablespoon cider vinegar
1 tablespoon vegetable oil
1 small jalapeño pepper, seeded and minced
½ teaspoon chili powder
¼ teaspoon dried thyme
Salt to taste

1. Arrange lettuce leaves on 4 salad plates. Overlap orange slices, onion rings, and avocado slices on lettuce.

2. For the dressing, mix lime juice, vinegar, oil, jalapeño, chili powder, thyme, and salt in a small bowl. Drizzle over each salad.

Red Cabbage Salad

Traditional German fare often means long cooking and heavy flavors. This easy salad, created for a Chicago Tribune "Fast Food" Oktoberfest menu, defies tradition. Red cabbage is enlivened with a tantalizing blend of raspberry vinegar, mango chutney, and Dijon mustard. If you don't have chutney on hand, try red currant jelly or other tart preserves.

½ medium head red cabbage

½ small red onion, cut into thin slivers

2 tablespoons plus 1½ teaspoons vegetable oil

2 tablespoons raspberry vinegar

1 teaspoon mango chutney

½ teaspoon Dijon mustard

¼ teaspoon sugar

¼ teaspoon ground pepper

Salt to taste

2 tablespoons minced toasted walnuts, see Note

2 tablespoons crumbled blue cheese

1. Toss cabbage and onion together in a large bowl. Combine oil, vinegar, chutney, mustard, sugar, pepper, and salt in a small bowl; mix well. Pour over cabbage mixture. Toss to combine. Sprinkle with walnuts and cheese.

Preparation time: 25 minutes

Yield: 4 servings

Nutrition information per serving:

Calories	135
Fat	12 g
Cholesterol	13 mg
Sodium	85 mg
Carbohydrate	6 g
Protein	3 g

NOTE

To toast walnuts, place them in a small skillet over medium heat. Cook and stir until golden, 1 to 2 minutes.

Ginger Coleslaw

Preparation time: 10 minutes

Yield: 6 servings

Nutrition information per
serving:

Calories	45
Fat	1 g
Cholesterol	1 mg
Sodium	40 mg
Carbohydrate	8 g
Protein	2 g

NOTE

Ginger preserves can be found
in the British foods area in
supermarkets or specialty
stores. A teaspoon of minced
gingerroot can be substituted.

*Traditional coleslaw undergoes a Pan-Asian update with the
addition of ginger, green onion, and rice vinegar. The ready-
made coleslaw mix makes this a quick-to-prepare recipe.*

1 16-ounce bag ready-to-use coleslaw mix
4 green onions, thinly sliced
2 tablespoons ginger preserves, see Note
2 tablespoons light mayonnaise
¼ cup seasoned rice vinegar
1 tablespoon fresh lemon or lime juice
Ground red pepper to taste

1. Combine coleslaw mix and green onions in a large bowl.

2. For the dressing, place preserves in the bowl of a small
   food processor fitted with a metal blade. Process until
   smooth. (Or strain through a mesh strainer; discard ginger pieces.) Add remaining ingredients to the processor;
   process just to mix. Pour dressing over coleslaw mix; toss
   well.

Peppered Broccoli Salad

Pine nuts, often associated with Italian dishes, have a delicate flavor—and a high price tag. But a little goes a long way. This Italian-accented salad from a Chicago Tribune "Fast Food" column uses only 1 tablespoon to good effect, sprinkled over broccoli flavored with red pepper and honey mustard. Look for broccoli florets at the supermarket salad bar.

12 ounces (4 cups) broccoli florets
1½ teaspoons olive oil
1½ teaspoons white-wine vinegar
½ teaspoon crushed red pepper flakes
¼ teaspoon honey mustard
¼ teaspoon salt
Pinch sugar
1 tablespoon toasted pine nuts, see Note

1. Cook broccoli in a large pan of boiling salted water just until crisp-tender, 3 to 5 minutes. Drain; rinse under cold water until cool. Pat dry; transfer to a bowl.

2. Whisk together remaining ingredients except pine nuts in a small bowl. Pour over broccoli; toss lightly. Sprinkle with pine nuts.

Preparation time: 5 minutes
Cooking time: 3 to 5 minutes
Yield: 4 servings

Nutrition information per serving:

Calories	55
Fat	3 g
Cholesterol	0 mg
Sodium	155 mg
Carbohydrate	5 g
Protein	3 g

NOTE

To toast the pine nuts, place in a small skillet over medium heat; cook and stir until golden, 1 to 2 minutes.

Moroccan Eggplant Salad

Preparation time: 30 minutes
Cooking time: 1½ to 2 hours
Yield: 8 servings

Nutrition information per serving:

Calories	175
Fat	15 g
Cholesterol	0 mg
Sodium	160 mg
Carbohydrate	13 g
Protein	1 g

For a story on brunch trends in the next millennium, caterer Lisa Gershenson of J&L Special Events and Corporate Food Management predicted that "the big change in brunch . . . will be its internationalization." A sterling example is her Moroccan eggplant salad served in Vietnamese crepe bundles. For an easier version, serve the salad in crispy baby lettuce leaf cups or store-bought crepes.

1 medium eggplant, cut into 1-inch cubes
1 medium red bell pepper, cut into 1-inch cubes
3 ribs celery, diced
1 small onion, chopped
3 plum tomatoes, chopped
2 cloves garlic, minced
½ cup olive oil
½ cup halved pitted green olives
¼ cup balsamic vinegar
¼ cup raisins
1 teaspoon ground cumin
1 teaspoon paprika
½ teaspoon cinnamon
½ teaspoon ground ginger
Salt to taste
Freshly ground black pepper to taste
Bibb lettuce leaves or ready-made crepes

1. Heat oven to 325°F. Stir together all ingredients except lettuce in 9″ × 13″ baking dish. Cover with foil; bake 30 minutes. Remove foil; continue baking until vegetables are very tender, 1 to 1½ hours.

2. Cool mixture. Season with salt and pepper. Serve in lettuce leaves or crepes.

Thai Fire-and-Ice Cucumber Salad

Opposites attract in this Thai-influenced salad, where the cooling flavor of cucumber and mint—chilled in a bowl of ice—joins forces with hot chilies. It is commonly served in small portions as a condiment for satay or other grilled meats. This recipe appeared in Pat Dailey's "Fast Food" column in the Chicago Tribune.

½ English or seedless cucumber, very thinly sliced
1 small sweet onion, such as Vidalia, thinly sliced and
   separated into rings
1 small hot red or green chili, thinly sliced
¼ teaspoon salt
Ice cubes
3 tablespoons seasoned rice vinegar
2 tablespoons chopped cilantro
1 tablespoon chopped fresh mint

1. Combine cucumber, onion, chili, and salt in a medium bowl. Cover with ice cubes; add enough water to cover. Let stand 10 minutes. Drain thoroughly; remove any remaining ice cubes.

2. Stir in vinegar, cilantro, and mint; serve.

Preparation time: 10 minutes
Standing time: 10 minutes
Yield: 4 servings

Nutrition information per serving:

Calories	15
Fat	0 g
Cholesterol	0 mg
Sodium	135 mg
Carbohydrate	3 g
Protein	1 g

Beet and Walnut Salad

Preparation time: 15 minutes
Cooking time: 1 hour
Chilling time: At least 1 hour
Yield: 6 servings

Nutrition information per serving:

Calories	130
Fat	9 g
Cholesterol	4 mg
Sodium	95 mg
Carbohydrate	13 g
Protein	3 g

Zakuska, a ritualized entertainment that dates back to eighteenth-century Russia, features an elaborate assortment of foods served buffet style. George Samutin, a native of Moscow, and his American wife, Valerie, prepare the time-consuming zakuska *table during the winter holidays. This beet salad with walnuts (salat iz krasnoy svyokly) is part of their menu—though it could be served any time of the year.*

1 pound whole small beets, stems and leaves cut away
3 large cloves garlic, minced
¼ cup chopped walnuts, or more to taste
¼ cup chopped prunes, or more to taste
3 tablespoons mayonnaise
Salt to taste

1. Heat oven to 375°F. Wrap each beet in foil; bake until fork-tender, about 1 hour. Let beets cool. Peel; shred with a grater or knife.

2. Combine beets, garlic, walnuts, prunes, mayonnaise, and salt in a medium bowl. Toss until mixed. Chill at least 1 hour. Remove from refrigerator 15 minutes before serving.

Tomato and Onion Salad with Oregano Dressing

This tomato and onion salad gets a punch from an Italian-inspired dressing that showcases oregano. Because the tomatoes take a starring role, use the best you can find. In the winter, imported tomatoes on the vine are more expensive but often taste riper than domestic tomatoes.

2 tablespoons red-wine vinegar
2 tablespoons extra-virgin olive oil
½ teaspoon dried oregano
Salt to taste
Freshly ground pepper to taste
2 small ribs celery, sliced ¼ inch thick
1 small sweet onion, quartered and sliced ¼ inch thick
3 ripe tomatoes, cut into wedges
Lettuce leaves for serving

1. Whisk vinegar, oil, oregano, salt, and pepper in a large bowl until blended.

2. Add celery and onion. Toss to coat. Stir in tomatoes. Serve on lettuce leaves.

Preparation time: 10 minutes
Yield: 4 servings

Nutrition information per serving:

Calories	90
Fat	7 g
Cholesterol	0 mg
Sodium	25 mg
Carbohydrate	7 g
Protein	1 g

Leek, Bean, Tomato, and Roquefort Salad

Preparation time: 25 minutes

Chilling time: 4 hours

Yield: 12 servings

Nutrition information per serving:

Calories	230
Fat	21 g
Cholesterol	42 mg
Sodium	385 mg
Carbohydrate	8 g
Protein	3 g

Caterer James Boardman shared this recipe for a French-influenced vegetable salad that combines leeks, wax beans, plum tomatoes, and Roquefort cheese. A tangy dressing uses tarragon, an aromatic herb that finds a home in many classic French dishes.

Dressing

2 egg yolks

¼ cup water

6 tablespoons red-wine vinegar

Juice and grated zest of 1 lemon

1 tablespoon minced fresh tarragon

1 teaspoon salt or to taste

½ teaspoon white pepper

1 cup extra-virgin olive oil

Salad

1 pound small leeks, cleaned and julienned

1 pound wax beans, trimmed and cooked until tender

1 pound plum tomatoes, cut in wedges

3 ounces Roquefort cheese, crumbled

2 tablespoons drained capers

1. For the dressing, combine yolks with ¼ cup water in the top of a double boiler or in a heavy saucepan. Cook over low heat, beating constantly with a handheld electric mixer or whisk, until the temperature reaches 160°F, about 15 to 20 minutes. Cool immediately in an ice bath or in the freezer. Combine egg yolks, vinegar, lemon juice and zest, tarragon, salt, and pepper in a blender; mix 1 minute. Slowly add oil while the blender is running; mix well.

2. Combine leeks, wax beans, and tomatoes in a large bowl. Add half of the dressing or to taste; toss lightly. Refrigerate at least 4 hours. Toss salad, adding more dressing if desired. Top with cheese and capers.

Roasted Pepper Salad with Goat Cheese and Oranges

This Mediterranean-inspired salad blends sweet onion, roasted bell peppers, and goat cheese. You can buy roasted peppers from a take-out shop or deli, or roast them yourself: Place peppers on a foil-lined baking sheet and place in the broiler, 6 to 8 inches from the flame; turn to blacken the skin on all sides. Place the charred peppers in a paper bag for about 10 minutes to cool; remove skins, then core and seed.

1 tablespoon plus 2 teaspoons olive oil

1 large Vidalia or other sweet onion, halved and cut in ¼-inch slices

3 tablespoons fresh orange juice

Salt to taste

Ground red pepper to taste

2 teaspoons minced fresh tarragon

4 bell peppers, a mix of red, yellow, and green, roasted, peeled, and seeded

1 tablespoon red-wine vinegar

4 large leaves red leaf lettuce

½ cup diced orange segments

¼ cup crumbled goat cheese

1. Heat 2 teaspoons oil in a nonstick skillet over high heat. Add onion wedges and cook, stirring often, until soft, 5 minutes. Add 1 tablespoon orange juice, salt, and a large dash of red pepper. Cook 1 minute, remove from heat; add 1 teaspoon tarragon. Set aside to cool.

2. Cut roasted peppers into strips. Combine with remaining 1 tablespoon oil, 2 tablespoons orange juice, and 1 teaspoon tarragon. Add vinegar, salt, and red pepper. Mix well.

3. Arrange lettuce on a serving plate; top with onion and pepper mixtures. Arrange orange pieces on top; sprinkle with goat cheese.

Preparation time: 30 minutes

Cooking time: 10 minutes

Yield: 6 servings

Nutrition information per serving:

Calories	95
Fat	6 g
Cholesterol	5 mg
Sodium	40 mg
Carbohydrate	8 g
Protein	3 g

Orzo Salad

Preparation time: 25 minutes
Cooking time: 15 minutes
Yield: 16 servings

*In an article offering alternatives to the iceberg-and-tomato rut,
Chicago Tribune food and wine columnist William Rice
suggested this Italian salad. It stars orzo, a tiny, rice-shaped
pasta that also is great in soups and can be used as a substitute
for rice. Note, too, the use of flat-leaf (or Italian) parsley, which
has a more intense flavor than curly parsley.*

Nutrition information per serving:

Calories	170
Fat	7 g
Cholesterol	0 mg
Sodium	105 mg
Carbohydrate	24 g
Protein	4 g

1 16-ounce box orzo
1 heaping tablespoon Dijon mustard with herbs
½ teaspoon salt
½ teaspoon freshly ground black pepper
¼ cup fresh lemon juice
2 tablespoons balsamic vinegar
¼ cup vegetable oil
3 tablespoons olive oil
½ red bell pepper, seeded and cubed
½ green bell pepper, seeded and cubed
½ medium onion, cubed
2 medium zucchini, cubed
1 small head napa cabbage, chopped
1 cup chopped fresh flat-leaf parsley

1. Cook orzo according to package directions until just tender, 12 to 15 minutes. Drain.

2. Combine mustard, salt, and pepper in a large bowl. Gradually stir in lemon juice and vinegar. Stir in oils.

3. Pour orzo into the bowl with dressing; toss. Add bell peppers, onion, zucchini, cabbage, and parsley; toss. Taste and adjust seasoning.

Pasta Salad with Tomato Compote

This pasta dish, developed for a Bastille Day column, gets a Parisian accent with shallots—tiny, delicately flavored onions that bear a closer resemblance to garlic. For the fresh herbs, consider using a blend often used in southern France: basil, fennel seed, lavender, marjoram, rosemary, sage, savory, and thyme.

1 9-ounce package fresh fettuccine, cooked according to
  package directions
3 tablespoons extra-virgin olive oil
1 tablespoon white-wine vinegar
2 medium shallots, minced
1 tablespoon drained capers
1 tablespoon whipping cream
1 teaspoon fresh lemon juice
Salt to taste
Ground red pepper to taste
3 tablespoons finely minced mixed fresh herbs
1 cup small cherry tomatoes, quartered lengthwise
1 small clove garlic, minced

1. Place hot, drained pasta in a large bowl; toss with 2 table-spoons plus 1½ teaspoons oil and the vinegar and shallots. Let stand until pasta is cool, about 10 minutes.

2. Add capers, cream, lemon juice, salt, red pepper, and herbs to pasta; mix well. Lightly toss tomatoes, garlic, remaining 1½ teaspoons oil, salt, and red pepper in a medium bowl.

3. Mound pasta on a small platter; place tomato mixture in the center. Serve at room temperature.

Preparation time: 25 minutes
Standing time: 10 minutes
Yield: 4 servings

Nutrition information per serving:

Calories	375
Fat	13 g
Cholesterol	5 mg
Sodium	55 mg
Carbohydrate	55 g
Protein	9 g

The Real Salad Niçoise

Preparation time: 45 minutes

Chilling time: 1 hour

Yield: 6 servings

Nutrition information per serving:

Calories	360
Fat	20 g
Cholesterol	115 mg
Sodium	495 mg
Carbohydrate	35 g
Protein	15 g

The idealized Mediterranean diet "sounds more like the way people eat at Chez Panisse (the Berkeley, California, restaurant) than the way they eat, and have traditionally eaten, around the Mediterranean," said Colman Andrews, author of Flavors of the Riviera. *So, if you travel to Nice, you won't be served a salad Niçoise with grilled rare tuna—it will be canned! Here's a recipe for the real McCoy, adapted from Andrews's book. Look for fava beans and baby artichokes in specialty produce stores or farmers' markets.*

10 firm medium tomatoes, quartered

Salt to taste

12 anchovy fillets or 2 6-ounce cans olive-oil-packed canned tuna, optional

1 pound fresh baby fava beans, shucked, or 12 baby artichokes, optional

1 clove garlic, cut in half lengthwise

1 cucumber, peeled and thinly sliced

2 green bell peppers, cored and thinly sliced

6 small onions, thinly sliced

3 hard-cooked eggs, quartered

3½ ounces Niçoise olives

6 tablespoons extra-virgin olive oil

6 fresh basil leaves, finely chopped

Freshly ground black pepper to taste

1. Place tomatoes on a platter; lightly salt. If using anchovies, cut each fillet into 3 or 4 pieces; if using tuna, drain and flake coarsely.

2. Blanch fava beans, if using, in boiling water 30 seconds; drain. Rinse well in cold water. Slip beans out of skins by grasping each one by its grooved end and squeezing gently. Cut stems off artichokes, if using; pull off tough outer leaves by hand. Trim a few more layers of leaves with a sharp knife. Scoop out chokes and cut artichokes into thin slices.

3. Rub bottom and sides of a large salad bowl with garlic pieces; discard garlic. Arrange anchovies or tuna, favas or artichokes, cucumber, green pepper, onions, eggs, and olives in the bowl. Drain tomatoes; salt again. Add to the bowl.

4. For the dressing, mix olive oil, basil, salt, and pepper in a small bowl. Refrigerate salad and dressing about 1 hour before serving; drizzle dressing over salad.

Asian Grilled Skirt Steak Salad

Preparation time: 15 minutes

Marinating time: 2 to 3 hours

Cooking time: 5 to 6 minutes

Yield: 4 to 6 servings

Chewy but flavorful, skirt steak stands up to being marinated, grilled, and sliced for this Asian-inspired salad of mixed greens dressed in soy sauce and rice vinegar.

Nutrition information per serving (based on 4):

Calories	340
Fat	21 g
Cholesterol	75 mg
Sodium	890 mg
Carbohydrate	5 g
Protein	32 g

Steak

1¼ pounds skirt steak

¼ cup soy sauce

¼ cup rice wine or dry white wine

2 tablespoons rice vinegar

2 teaspoons peeled, minced gingerroot

¼ cup finely chopped green onions

Salad

8 cups mixed lettuces such as mesclun

½ teaspoon five-spice powder

½ teaspoon freshly ground pepper

1 tablespoon soy sauce

1 tablespoon rice wine vinegar

1 tablespoon balsamic vinegar

3 tablespoons vegetable oil

1. Cut steak in half crosswise and place in a shallow dish just large enough to hold the meat in a single layer. Combine soy sauce, rice wine, rice vinegar, ginger, and green onions in a small bowl. Stir well; pour over meat. Cover and refrigerate 2 to 3 hours, turning steaks once.

2. For the salad, place lettuces in a large salad bowl. Combine five-spice powder and pepper in a small bowl. Stir in soy sauce; add rice wine and vinegar and slowly stir in oil. Set dressing aside.

3. Prepare grill or heat broiler. Remove meat from marinade; pat dry. Grill or broil meat, 6 inches from heat source, until one side is browned, about 3 minutes. Turn; cook 2 minutes for medium rare or 3 minutes for medium. Transfer the steaks to a cutting board. Allow to rest 5 minutes. Cut across the grain on a diagonal into thin slices.

4. Pour dressing over lettuces; toss. Arrange a bed of salad on plates; top with sliced skirt steak.

Italian Shrimp and Fennel Salad

Preparation time: 35 minutes
Cooking time: 10 minutes
Yield: 4 servings

Nutrition information per serving:

Calories	224
Fat	10 g
Cholesterol	225 mg
Sodium	301 mg
Carbohydrate	9 g
Protein	26 g

This salad delivers a delicious, fresh flavor that's perfect for warm-weather dining. The shrimp and vegetables gain a flavor boost from garlic and fresh rosemary.

2 tablespoons plus 1½ teaspoons olive oil
1 large red bell pepper, diced
1 medium fennel bulb, trimmed and diced
¼ teaspoon crushed red pepper flakes
Salt to taste
Juice of 1 large lemon
1 pound large shrimp, peeled and deveined
1 small clove garlic, minced
3 green onions, sliced
1 tablespoon drained capers
1 teaspoon reduced-fat mayonnaise
2 to 3 teaspoons minced fresh rosemary

1. Heat 1 tablespoon oil in a large skillet over high heat. Add bell pepper, fennel, ⅛ teaspoon crushed pepper flakes, and salt to taste. Cook, stirring often, until vegetables begin to brown at edges, 6 to 7 minutes. Transfer to a large bowl; add half of the lemon juice.

2. Heat the additional 1 tablespoon oil in the same skillet. Add shrimp, remaining ⅛ teaspoon pepper flakes, and salt to taste. Cook, stirring, until shrimp are pink, 2 to 3 minutes. Add remaining lemon juice and garlic. Add mixture to vegetables.

3. Add remaining 1½ teaspoons oil and the green onions, capers, mayonnaise, and rosemary; mix well. Cool to room temperature or refrigerate overnight. Adjust seasoning at serving time.

Entrees

Alicia's, Milwaukee Avenue

Moroccan Salmon with Tomato-Mint Relish

Preparation time: 20 minutes

Cooking time: 10 minutes

Yield: 4 servings

Nutrition information per serving:

Calories	220
Fat	11 g
Cholesterol	65 mg
Sodium	60 mg
Carbohydrate	5 g
Protein	25 g

Chicago Tribune *"Fast Food"* columnist Pat Dailey borrowed *from the Moroccan spice cabinet for this stylish salmon dish. She recommended serving it with Chive Couscous (see Index).*

1 tablespoon olive oil

½ teaspoon hot paprika

¼ teaspoon ground cumin

⅛ teaspoon ground coriander

Salt to taste

Ground red pepper to taste

4 salmon fillets

3 plum tomatoes, diced

2 green onions, sliced

3 tablespoons orange juice

2 tablespoons minced fresh mint

1. Pour oil into a large skillet; stir in paprika, cumin, coriander, salt, and red pepper. Heat over high heat. Add salmon; sear on both sides. Reduce heat to medium; continue cooking until salmon is cooked through, 6 to 7 minutes. Set aside on plates; keep warm.

2. Add tomatoes, green onions, and orange juice to skillet. Cook, stirring until hot, 1 minute. Add mint; remove from heat. Spoon over salmon and serve.

Sautéed Monkfish in Wasabi Broth

The culinary pleasures of a little pain were the takeoff point for a Chicago Tribune *story on fiery seasonings in 1997. This recipe takes wasabi paste from its pigeonhole as a sushi sidekick and uses it to heat up a fish fillet. The dish is adapted from one by Don Yamauchi, chef at Gordon restaurant in Chicago.*

Preparation time: 15 minutes
Cooking time: 4 to 5 minutes
Yield: 4 servings

4 monkfish or other firm white fish fillets, about
  4 ounces each
Salt to taste
Freshly ground black pepper to taste
¼ cup wasabi paste
1 cup all-purpose flour
1 tablespoon salt
1 teaspoon ground red pepper
1 teaspoon ground coriander
2 tablespoons butter
Olive oil
½ cup water
½ cup reduced-sodium soy sauce

Nutrition information per serving:

Calories	345
Fat	13 g
Cholesterol	45 mg
Sodium	1,480 mg
Carbohydrate	33 g
Protein	21 g

NOTE

Look for wasabi in Asian food shops; if you only find powdered wasabi, make a paste by adding a small amount of water.

1. Season fish with salt and pepper; place on a plate. Coat fillets on both sides with 2 tablespoons of wasabi.

2. Mix together flour, salt, red pepper, and coriander on another plate. Place fish in flour mixture to coat both sides; shake off excess.

3. Heat butter and enough olive oil to cover the bottom of a large skillet over medium heat. Cook fish, turning once, 3 to 4 minutes or until golden brown.

4. Meanwhile, heat water and the soy sauce together in a saucepan. Whisk in remaining wasabi paste. Place monkfish in a serving bowl and spoon broth around. Serve warm.

Pan-Fried Sea Bass with Phoenix Sauce

Preparation time: 15 minutes

Cooking time: 8 minutes

Yield: 4 servings

Nutrition information per serving:

Calories	240
Fat	11 g
Cholesterol	60 mg
Sodium	505 mg
Carbohydrate	5 g
Protein	28 g

This recipe is adapted from one used at Phoenix Restaurant in Chicago's Chinatown around the Chinese New Year. Fish is so essential to a new year's feast that in provinces where it is scarce, cooks carve a fish from wood, cover it with a flour-and-water paste, and deep-fry it; diners eat just the shell.

Sauce

1 cup unsalted chicken broth

1 tablespoon cornstarch

3 teaspoons light soy sauce

1 teaspoon sugar

1 teaspoon dark soy sauce

1 teaspoon oyster sauce

¼ teaspoon sesame oil

Fish

1 pound sea bass fillets

2 tablespoons plus 1 teaspoon vegetable oil

1 shallot, finely chopped

1 clove garlic, minced

1 small rib celery, finely chopped

1 tablespoon minced gingerroot

1. Combine sauce ingredients in a small bowl; set aside.

2. Fry sea bass fillets in a skillet with 2 tablespoons oil until golden brown and cooked through, about 7 minutes. Remove to a warm serving platter. Set aside.

3. Heat remaining 1 teaspoon oil in a small saucepan. Add shallot, garlic, celery, and ginger; cook 2 minutes. Stir sauce mix; add to pan. Cook, stirring, until thickened. Serve sauce over warm fish.

Coconut Shrimp Curry with Peas

As supermarkets stock new convenience foods such as curry and pasta sauces, pesto, and seasoning bases, cooking the same pasta, rice, and chicken can be quick as well as adventurous.

Preparation time: 45 minutes
Cooking time: 20 minutes
Yield: 4 servings

1 teaspoon vegetable oil
1 onion, chopped
1 large red bell pepper, seeded and chopped
2 cloves garlic, minced
1 to 2 jalapeño peppers, seeded and thinly sliced
  lengthwise
3 tablespoons bottled curry sauce
½ teaspoon ground cumin
½ cup 2 percent milk
½ cup unsweetened coconut milk, see Note
1 pound large shrimp, peeled and deveined, tails left on if
  desired
½ cup frozen peas
Salt to taste
Freshly ground pepper to taste
3 cups cooked white rice
Chopped cilantro, fresh lime wedges for garnish

Nutrition information per serving:

Calories	440
Fat	11 g
Cholesterol	170 mg
Sodium	295 mg
Carbohydrate	57 g
Protein	27 g

1. Heat oil in a large, heavy saucepan over medium heat. Add onion and bell pepper. Cook, stirring, until softened, about 5 minutes. Add garlic, jalapeños, curry sauce, and cumin; cook, stirring, until aromatic, about 2 minutes.

2. Reduce heat to low; stir in milk and coconut milk. Simmer, stirring, 5 minutes. Stir in shrimp; cook, stirring occasionally, just until shrimp are cooked through, 3 to 5 minutes. Stir in peas, salt, and pepper; heat.

3. Serve curry in wide bowls with a scoop of rice; sprinkle cilantro over. Pass lime wedges for squeezing over curry.

NOTE
Cans of unsweetened coconut milk can be found in the Asian section of some supermarkets; freeze leftovers in ice cube trays to use later.

Big Bowl's Singapore Chili Shrimp and Rice

Preparation time: 1 hour

Cooking time: 15 minutes

Yield: 2 servings

Nutrition information per serving (with 2 tablespoons sauce):

Calories	360
Fat	11 g
Cholesterol	60 mg
Sodium	790 mg
Carbohydrate	54 g
Protein	12 g

One-dish cooking extends well beyond the expected stews and soups, especially when cooks follow the lead of bowl-crazy restaurateurs such as Matt McMillin, executive chef of Big Bowl in Chicago. "It's a food philosophy that embraces variety, convenience, economy, and really fresh food," he said in a 1997 story. This simple but sumptuous stir-fry is his most popular special. He recommends flavorful jasmine rice, sold at Asian markets, natural-food stores, and some supermarkets. Any brand of chili paste will work.

Chili Sauce

2 teaspoons peanut oil

2 tablespoons chopped gingerroot

1½ pounds fresh ripe tomatoes, peeled, seeded, and chopped, or 1 14-ounce can crushed tomatoes

2 tablespoons sugar

2½ teaspoons Japanese soy sauce

2½ teaspoons prepared chili paste

¾ teaspoon salt

Shrimp

1 tablespoon peanut oil

10 large fresh shrimp, peeled, deveined, and butterflied

1 tablespoon minced gingerroot

1 tablespoon minced garlic

1¼ cups cooked jasmine or long grain rice

1 baby bok choy, blanched, drained, and sliced

2 cilantro sprigs

8 drops Asian sesame oil

1 lime wedge

1. For the sauce, heat oil in a large skillet over medium heat. Add ginger; cook 20 seconds. Add tomatoes and heat to a simmer. Cook the mixture until thickened, about 10 minutes. Add sugar, soy sauce, chili paste, and salt. Cook to blend flavors, 1 to 2 minutes. Set aside. (Refrigerate excess sauce for other uses.)

2. For shrimp, heat peanut oil in medium skillet over medium heat. Add shrimp and cook 20 seconds. Add ginger and garlic; cook 15 to 20 seconds. Add ¾ cup of the reserved chili sauce and simmer until shrimp are just cooked, about 2½ minutes.

3. Pour shrimp mixture over cooked rice in large serving bowl. Garnish with bok choy, cilantro sprigs, sesame oil, and lime wedge.

Grilled Caribbean Curried Shrimp

Preparation time: 1 hour

Chilling time: 1 hour

Cooking time: 20 minutes

Yield: 4 servings

Nutrition information per serving (using all the sauce):

Calories	460
Fat	31 g
Cholesterol	165 mg
Sodium	480 mg
Carbohydrate	23 g
Protein	26 g

Monique King, chef at Soul Kitchen in Chicago's Wicker Park neighborhood, created a summer entree that has what she calls a "strong citrus connection." The shrimp marinate in a bath of spiced coconut milk before going on the grill, and afterward are adorned with a curry sauce of orange juice and coconut milk spiked with chilies, ginger, and garlic. Serve the shrimp with rice on the side.

Marinade and Shrimp

2 tablespoons olive oil

10 cloves garlic, chopped

1 2-inch piece gingerroot, peeled and chopped

½ red onion, chopped

2 teaspoons ground turmeric

¼ teaspoon red pepper

¾ cup unsweetened coconut milk

1 to 1¼ pounds medium shrimp, washed, peeled with tails left on, and deveined

Sauce

1 tablespoon vegetable oil

½ red onion, minced

3 cloves garlic, minced

1 ½-inch piece gingerroot, peeled and minced

Zest of 2 oranges

Zest of 1 lime

Zest of 1 lemon

1 teaspoon cumin powder

¼ teaspoon red pepper

2 teaspoons ground turmeric

2 teaspoons curry powder

Salt to taste

Freshly ground black pepper to taste

1½ cups orange juice

3 cups fish stock or 2 cups clam juice mixed with 1 cup
  water
1 13½-ounce can unsweetened coconut milk
1½ cups diced tomato or 1 16-ounce can diced tomatoes,
  drained
Lime wedges for garnish

1. For the marinade, combine oil, garlic, ginger, onion, turmeric, and red pepper in the bowl of a food processor; puree. Pour in coconut milk. Combine marinade and shrimp in a stainless steel or glass bowl. Cover with plastic wrap; refrigerate at least 1 hour, up to 8 hours.

2. Soak several small wooden skewers in water 20 minutes. For the sauce, heat oil in a skillet. Add onion, garlic, and ginger; cook 1 minute. Add zests, cumin, red pepper, turmeric, and curry powder. Stir over low heat 30 seconds; pour in orange juice. Boil until the liquid is reduced by half. Add fish stock, coconut milk, and tomatoes. Simmer 15 minutes.

3. Prepare grill or heat broiler. Remove shrimp from marinade; thread on skewers, allowing 3 or 4 to a skewer. Grill or broil 6 inches from heat source, turning once, until shrimp are pink, 3 to 4 minutes.

4. Make a pool of hot sauce on four warm plates; place skewers on sauce, dividing equally among plates. Garnish with lime wedges.

Daniel J's Penne with Chicken, Smoked Mozzarella, Dried Tomatoes, and Spinach

Preparation time: 45 minutes

Chilling time: 1 hour or
    overnight

Cooking time: 12 minutes

Yield: 8 servings

Nutrition information per serving:

Calories	495
Fat	16 g
Cholesterol	70 mg
Sodium	315 mg
Carbohydrate	49 g
Protein	39 g

Smoked mozzarella is the finishing touch on this Italian-influenced creation. Jack Daniel Jones, chef-owner of Daniel J's restaurant on the North Side of Chicago, uses one pot and one skillet before mixing this recipe in a single big bowl. He grills the marinated chicken breasts over hardwood before completing the dish, a step you can skip. (One step you shouldn't skip: Scoop out a cup of pasta cooking water before draining the pasta, to use for moistening the sauced pasta if it turns out too dry.)

Marinade and Chicken

2 tablespoons extra-virgin olive oil

2 tablespoons chopped fresh basil

1 tablespoon chopped fresh chives

1 tablespoon chopped fresh thyme

1 tablespoon chopped red onion

2 cloves garlic, minced

Salt to taste

Freshly ground pepper to taste

6 boneless, skinless chicken breast halves, cubed

Pasta

1 pound penne or other tubular pasta

2 tablespoons extra-virgin olive oil

2 tablespoons minced shallots

2 large cloves garlic, minced

¼ cup dry white wine

2 pounds ripe plum tomatoes, peeled, seeded, and chopped, or 1 14½-ounce can diced tomatoes in juice

12 oil-packed sun-dried tomato halves, patted dry and julienned

½ cup chicken broth

1 1-pound bag fresh spinach

½ pound smoked mozzarella, diced
Salt to taste
Freshly ground black pepper to taste
Red pepper flakes to taste, optional

1. Combine olive oil, basil, chives, thyme, onion, garlic, salt, and pepper in a nonreactive bowl; add chicken. Toss to coat. Cover; refrigerate at least 1 hour or overnight. Drain off marinade.

2. Cook pasta according to package directions. Meanwhile, heat olive oil over high heat in a 12-inch nonstick skillet. Add chicken; cook, stirring occasionally, until chicken begins to brown, 3 to 4 minutes. Add shallots; cook 30 seconds. Add garlic; cook until golden, 3 to 4 minutes.

3. Add white wine to pan; stir, scraping bottom to loosen caramelized bits. Add tomatoes. Heat to a boil. Stir in dried tomatoes and chicken broth. Lower heat; simmer, stirring frequently, until sauce thickens, about 5 minutes. Add spinach, stirring just until wilted.

4. Drain pasta; place in a large serving bowl. Add chicken mixture and mozzarella. Toss until cheese begins to melt. Season with salt, black pepper, and red pepper flakes.

Costa Rican Rice with Chicken

Preparation time: 30 minutes
Cooking time: 50 minutes
Yield: 6 servings

Nutrition information per serving:

Calories	325
Fat	5 g
Cholesterol	45 mg
Sodium	535 mg
Carbohydrate	44 g
Protein	24 g

A Chicago Tribune potluck contest drew some fine entries, including this one from Laura M. Kochevar. She encountered arroz con pollo (rice with chicken) while she served as a Peace Corps volunteer in Costa Rica in the late 1980s. "It is the typical dish served on Sundays, at weddings, baptisms, birthday parties, showers, and other special events," she said. This more healthful version uses a limited amount of oil, skinless chicken, and lots of cilantro. Sazon, a Spanish seasoning mix, such as Goya brand, is available in the ethnic section of large supermarkets or in Latin food shops.

1 pound boneless chicken breasts
1 tablespoon oil
1½ cups rice
1 onion, chopped
1 clove garlic, minced
1 red bell pepper, chopped
1 envelope sazon seasoning
½ cup chopped cilantro plus more for garnish
2 tablespoons uncooked peas or capers, optional
Salt to taste

1. Heat 4 cups water to a boil in a saucepan; add chicken. Reduce heat to simmer; cook until done, about 30 minutes. Remove chicken; skim fat from broth. Reserve 3 cups broth for cooking rice. Remove skin from chicken; shred meat into bite-sized pieces.

2. Heat oil in a large, heavy pot. Add rice, onion, garlic, and red pepper; cook, stirring, 2 minutes. Add chicken broth and seasoning mix. Cover; cook over low heat until rice is tender, about 15 minutes. Mix in chicken, cilantro, and peas or capers. Salt to taste. Serve in a large bowl; sprinkle with chopped cilantro.

Herb Roasted Chicken

The boom in American versions of the French brasserie has revived such hearty, simple favorites as roast chicken. This recipe is adapted from one by chefs Gale Gand and Rick Tramonto of Brasserie T in Northfield, Illinois.

1 small whole chicken or 1 large Cornish hen, about
    1¼ pounds
2 tablespoons unsalted butter, softened
2 cloves garlic, minced
1 tablespoon mixed chopped fresh herbs, such as parsley,
    chives, chervil, tarragon, or thyme, plus more for
    garnish
3 tablespoons olive oil
About ½ teaspoon coarse (kosher) salt or to taste
Freshly ground pepper to taste

1. Heat oven to 400°F. Rinse chicken; pat dry. Mix butter, 1 clove garlic, and 1 tablespoon chopped herbs in a small dish. Use fingers to loosen skin away from chicken flesh. Spread butter mixture under the skin and over the chicken flesh.

2. Mix 1 tablespoon oil and remaining 1 clove garlic; spread over outside of chicken. Sprinkle with salt and pepper.

3. Heat remaining 2 tablespoons oil in an ovenproof skillet over medium-high heat. Add chicken; sear, turning frequently, until browned on all sides, about 10 minutes. Place pan in oven; cook until skin is crisp and juices from the thigh run clear, about 30 minutes. Serve sprinkled with additional chopped fresh herbs.

Preparation time: 45 minutes
Cooking time: 40 minutes
Yield: 2 servings

Nutrition information per serving:

Calories	575
Fat	39 g
Cholesterol	185 mg
Sodium	610 mg
Carbohydrate	2 g
Protein	52 g

Paella

Preparation time: 1 hour
Cooking time: 1½ hours
Yield: 8 servings

Nutrition information per serving:

Calories	485
Fat	21 g
Cholesterol	95 mg
Sodium	670 mg
Carbohydrate	43 g
Protein	29 g

Spanish paella, perhaps the world's best rice casserole, is worth the time it takes to make; it's a true show-stopper. Vary the meats and seafoods to make the dish your own. Paella is meant to be cooked fairly quickly on top of the stove, so its pan must be shallow and broad. Restaurant paella pans are usually carbon steel and have two loop handles. Others are made of clay, copper, stainless steel, or enameled steel.

2 tablespoons olive oil plus more as needed
1 broiler/fryer chicken, cut up
6 to 8 small fully cooked pork sausages, Spanish chorizo, or garlic sausages
12 to 16 large shrimp, peeled and deveined
6 to 8 very small lobster tails, shelled and halved, optional
3 onions, chopped
4 plum tomatoes, peeled, seeded, and chopped
4 cloves garlic, minced
2 tablespoons chopped fresh parsley or cilantro
10 to 15 saffron threads, crushed
4 cups chicken broth, or more if needed
1 pound short-grain rice, such as arborio, about 2 cups
3 small red bell peppers, seeded and cut into ¼-inch strips
1 cup dry white wine
12 to 16 mussels, cleaned
½ cup fresh peas or frozen peas, unthawed
Salt to taste
Freshly ground black pepper to taste
Chopped fresh parsley for garnish

1. Heat olive oil in a paella pan or very large, heavy skillet over medium-high heat. Add chicken pieces and cook until browned, 10 to 15 minutes. Remove to paper towels to drain. Add sausages to pan. Cook until browned; remove to paper towels to drain. Add more oil to the pan, if needed. Cook shrimp, stirring, until almost pink. Drain on paper towels. Cook lobster until almost tender, about 5 minutes. Drain on paper towels.

2. Add onions to the same pan and cook, stirring frequently, until soft, about 5 minutes. Stir in tomatoes, garlic, parsley, and saffron. Cook, stirring often, 2 minutes. Add 1 cup chicken broth; heat to a boil. Reduce heat; simmer 10 minutes.

3. Return chicken to the pan; top with rice and red peppers. Pour wine and remaining 3 cups broth over rice. Increase heat to medium; boil, stirring occasionally, until half the liquid is absorbed, 15 to 20 minutes. Add sausage, mussels, and peas. Reduce heat to medium; simmer until mussels have opened, rice is tender, and liquid is absorbed, about 18 minutes. Add more broth if rice needs longer cooking. Season with salt and black pepper. Arrange shrimp and lobster over rice; heat until warm. Remove from heat; let sit 10 minutes. Sprinkle with parsley.

Chicken Vesuvio

Preparation time: 25 minutes
Cooking time: 50 minutes
Yield: 4 servings

Nutrition information per
serving:

Calories	680
Fat	46 g
Cholesterol	130 mg
Sodium	415 mg
Carbohydrate	30 g
Protein	35 g

Chicken Vesuvio is a true Chicago original and is served in many of the Italian restaurants in town. It's fried and then baked with plenty of garlic, olive oil, and potatoes.

1 broiler/fryer chicken, about 3 pounds, cut up
⅓ cup all-purpose flour
1½ teaspoons dried basil
¾ teaspoon dried oregano
½ teaspoon salt
¼ teaspoon dried thyme
¼ teaspoon freshly ground pepper
Pinch dried rosemary
Pinch rubbed sage
½ cup olive oil
3 baking potatoes, cut into lengthwise wedges
3 tablespoons chopped fresh parsley
3 cloves garlic, minced
¾ cup dry white wine

1. Rinse chicken under cold water; pat dry. Mix flour, basil, oregano, salt, thyme, pepper, rosemary, and sage in a shallow dish. Roll chicken in flour mixture. Shake off excess.

2. Heat oil in a 12-inch cast-iron or other ovenproof skillet over medium-high heat until hot. Add chicken pieces in a single layer. Fry in batches, if necessary, turning occasionally, until browned on all sides, about 15 minutes. Remove to paper towels.

3. Add potato wedges to the skillet. Fry, turning occasionally, until light brown on all sides. Remove and drain on paper towels.

4. Heat oven to 375°F. Pour off all but 2 tablespoons fat from the skillet. Put chicken and potatoes back into the skillet. Sprinkle with parsley and garlic. Pour wine over all.

5. Bake, covered, 10 minutes. Uncover; bake until potatoes are fork-tender and thigh juices run clear, 15 to 20 minutes. Let stand 5 minutes before serving. Serve with a little of the pan juices.

Mediterranean Chicken with Cucumber Sauce and Couscous

Preparation time: 1 hour
Marinating time: Overnight
Cooking time: 20 minutes
Yield: 12 servings

Nutrition information per serving:

Calories	520
Fat	25 g
Cholesterol	127 mg
Sodium	577 mg
Carbohydrate	31 g
Protein	39 g

Mediterranean cooking is deliciously varied, drawing inspiration from the kitchens of Greece, southern Italy, southern France, Spain, Turkey, and the countries of North Africa—Morocco, Algeria, and Tunisia. Here marinated chicken is grilled, then served with couscous, a granular pasta, and a yogurt-cucumber sauce.

Marinade and Chicken
1 bunch cilantro, coarsely chopped
8 green onions, including greens, thinly sliced
8 cloves garlic, chopped
¼ cup fennel seeds, toasted and crushed
2 tablespoons grated gingerroot
2 tablespoons salt
2 tablespoons hot Hungarian paprika
2 teaspoons ground red pepper
2 teaspoons ground cumin
1 cup olive oil
¾ cup fresh lemon juice
24 chicken thighs, skin on

Sauce
1 cucumber, peeled and diced
4 cups plain yogurt
6 cloves garlic, minced
½ cup coarsely chopped fresh dill
Juice of 2 lemons
Salt to taste
Red pepper to taste

Couscous
2 cups chicken broth
2 cups couscous
1 medium carrot, peeled and finely diced

1 small red onion, peeled and finely diced
1 rib celery, finely diced
¼ cup finely chopped fresh parsley
Juice of 1 lemon
Salt to taste
Freshly ground black pepper to taste

1. For the marinade, mix cilantro, onions, garlic, fennel, ginger, salt, paprika, red pepper, cumin, olive oil, and lemon juice in a nonmetallic bowl. Add chicken; toss to coat pieces well. Cover; refrigerate overnight.

2. For the sauce, place all ingredients in a nonmetallic bowl; mix thoroughly. Cover; refrigerate overnight.

3. Prepare a grill or broiler. Remove chicken pieces from marinade, letting excess marinade drip off. Grill or broil 6 inches from heat source, turning frequently so chicken does not burn, until done, about 15 to 20 minutes, depending on the heat of the grill.

4. For the couscous, heat broth in a medium saucepan to a simmer. Slowly stir in couscous; remove saucepan from heat. Cover; let stand 5 minutes. Place couscous into a serving bowl; fluff with a fork. Add carrot, onion, celery, parsley, and lemon juice; toss gently to mix. Adjust seasoning with salt and pepper. Place couscous on 12 plates; top with 2 thighs per plate. Serve cucumber sauce over top or on the side.

Grilled Chicken with Pickled Cabbage Salad

Preparation time: 40 minutes

Marinating time: 30 minutes

Cooking time: 10 minutes

Yield: 4 servings

Nutrition information per serving:

Calories	340
Fat	26 g
Cholesterol	35 mg
Sodium	60 mg
Carbohydrate	14 g
Protein	16 g

The food of South America remains largely overlooked by North Americans. Restaurants often introduce ethnic cuisines to new audiences, but few South American dishes have pioneered their way north. This Peruvian chicken can be served as a main course, using one breast half per serving or presented as part of a tapas-style meal. The optional annatto seeds, also called achiote, *provide the dish's deep color. Look for them in Latin markets.*

Chicken
¼ cup olive oil

2 teaspoons annatto seeds, optional

1 teaspoon cumin seeds

1 small clove garlic, minced

⅓ cup red-wine vinegar

1 hot chili, seeded if desired and minced

Salt to taste

Black pepper to taste

2 whole boneless, skinless chicken breasts, split

Cabbage Salad
4 cups finely shredded cabbage

½ red bell pepper, cut in thin strips

½ green bell pepper, cut in thin strips

2 green onions, cut in slivers

1 hot chili, seeded, cut in thin slivers

½ cup chopped cilantro

½ cup cider vinegar

1 tablespoon water

2 teaspoons sugar

¼ teaspoon chili powder

Hot red pepper sauce to taste

Salt to taste

Freshly ground black pepper to taste
3 tablespoons vegetable oil
Lime wedges for serving

1. Combine olive oil, annatto seeds, cumin seeds, and garlic in a small saucepan. Cook gently until oil turns deep gold, about 5 minutes. Remove from heat; cool to room temperature; strain out seeds.

2. Stir vinegar, chili, salt, and black pepper into oil. Transfer to a large plastic food storage bag; add chicken. Seal bag and turn it over several times so the chicken is well coated. Refrigerate 30 minutes.

3. Meanwhile, for cabbage salad, combine cabbage, bell pepper, green onions, chili, and cilantro in a large bowl. Mix vinegar, water, sugar, chili powder, hot pepper sauce, salt, and black pepper in a separate bowl. Add oil; mix well. Toss dressing with cabbage mixture; adjust seasoning. Cabbage salad can be made a day ahead of time and refrigerated. Mix well before serving.

4. Prepare grill to medium-high heat or heat broiler. Remove chicken from marinade. Grill or broil, 4 inches from heat, for 5 minutes. Turn and cook 5 minutes until cooked throughout. Serve chicken hot or at room temperature over cabbage. Pass lime wedges; squeeze fresh lime juice to taste over chicken.

Spicy Tangerine Chicken with Bok Choy

Preparation time: 35 minutes

Cooking time: 8 minutes

Yield: 4 servings

Nutrition information per serving:

Calories	205
Fat	6 g
Cholesterol	65 mg
Sodium	240 mg
Carbohydrate	8 g
Protein	28 g

Wok cooking offers a speedy route to a fresh, healthful weekday meal. This dish makes use of flavored cooking oils that are widely available; any of the Asian types would work, like lemongrass-flavored oil, cilantro oil, even lemon pepper oil. Vegetable oil can be used; just be sure to increase other seasonings.

1 teaspoon minced tangerine zest

½ to ¾ teaspoon red pepper flakes

6 tablespoons tangerine juice

3 tablespoons seasoned rice vinegar

2 teaspoons reduced-sodium soy sauce

1 pound boneless, skinless chicken breasts, cut into ¾-inch slices

4 teaspoons vegetable oil, preferably an Asian flavored variety

1 large sweet onion, cut into 12 wedges

1 small (about 12-ounce) head bok choy, bias-cut into ¾-inch pieces

1. Heat a wok or heavy skillet over high heat. Add tangerine zest and ¼ teaspoon red pepper flakes. Cook, stirring frequently, until fragrant, 45 seconds. Transfer to a medium bowl. Add 2 tablespoons tangerine juice, 1 tablespoon vinegar, and 1 teaspoon soy sauce. Stir in chicken; toss to coat. Set aside. (Chicken can marinate up to 4 hours in the refrigerator.)

2. Combine remaining 4 tablespoons juice, 2 tablespoons vinegar, and 1 teaspoon soy sauce with ¼ teaspoon red pepper flakes in a small bowl; set sauce aside.

3. Heat 2 teaspoons oil in a wok over high heat, adding ¼ teaspoon red pepper flakes if a hotter dish is desired. Add chicken; stir-fry just until no longer pink, about 2 minutes. Remove from wok; set aside. Heat remaining 2 teaspoons oil in the wok. Add onion and bok choy; stir-fry until crisp-tender, 2 to 3 minutes, adding half of the reserved sauce to the pan after 1 minute. Return chicken to the pan along with remaining sauce. Cook briefly, just until heated through.

Colombian Chicken and Potato Stew

Preparation time: 45 minutes

Cooking time: 20 minutes

Yield: 6 servings

Nutrition information per serving:

Calories	415
Fat	15 g
Cholesterol	95 mg
Sodium	1,165 mg
Carbohydrate	39 g
Protein	32 g

Potatoes are an important crop in Colombia. This stew includes just two of the most common types, although you can add as many as you like. For the chicken, buying a rotisserie version is the easiest option, although leftover chicken or turkey also can be used.

5 cups chicken broth

1 dried red chili, such as guajillo, optional

3 small red potatoes, unpeeled and cut in 1-inch chunks

3 Yukon Gold potatoes, unpeeled and cut in 1-inch chunks

1 large sweet potato, cut in 1-inch chunks

1 large onion, cut in 1-inch chunks

½ pound ready-cut carrots

½ teaspoon ground coriander

½ teaspoon salt

½ teaspoon coarsely ground black pepper

1 cooked chicken, skinned and boned, meat torn in pieces

2 small ears corn, each cut into 3 pieces

⅓ cup whipping cream, optional

¼ cup minced cilantro

1 avocado, peeled, diced

1 tablespoon plus 1½ teaspoons drained capers

1. Put broth and chili, if using, in a large pot; place over medium-high heat. Add potatoes, sweet potato, onion, carrots, coriander, salt, and black pepper. Heat to a boil. Cover; reduce heat to low. Simmer 10 minutes.

2. Add chicken and corn. Continue to cook until potatoes are tender, 5 to 8 minutes. Add cream and cilantro; adjust seasoning. Serve in bowls; garnish with avocado and capers.

Sautéed Duck Breast with Pan-Asian Flavors

Chicago Tribune *food writer Pat Dailey came up with this gingery-sweet sauce for sautéed duck breast, which is increasingly available in supermarkets. For a leaner version, you can make the sauce without cream. If you do so, you may wish to reduce the sauce a little further to intensify the flavor. Substitute 1 teaspoon grated lemon zest for the lemongrass, if you like.*

1 tablespoon unsalted butter
4 boneless duck breast halves, skin removed
Salt to taste
Freshly ground pepper to taste
1 stalk lemongrass, minced
1 piece (½-inch) gingerroot, minced
⅓ cup chicken broth
⅓ cup sweet white wine
1 tablespoon seasoned rice vinegar
1 tablespoon orange marmalade
¼ cup whipping cream

Preparation time: 20 minutes
Cooking time: 14 minutes
Yield: 4 servings

Nutrition information per serving:

Calories	300
Fat	16 g
Cholesterol	155 mg
Sodium	170 mg
Carbohydrate	4 g
Protein	34 g

1. Melt butter in a large skillet over medium-high heat. Add duck breasts; season with salt and pepper. Cook, turning once or twice, until cooked as desired. Remove from pan and set aside; cover to keep warm.

2. Add lemongrass, ginger, broth, wine, vinegar, and marmalade to the pan. Cook over high heat until reduced by half, about 5 minutes. Strain into a small dish. Wipe out the pan with a paper towel.

3. Return the sauce mixture to the skillet; add cream. Boil until it is thickened to coat the back of a wooden spoon, about 3 to 4 minutes. Add salt and pepper to taste. Slice the duck breasts on a diagonal and fan the slices on dinner plates. Drizzle lightly with the sauce.

Duck with Onion Sauce

Preparation time: 40 minutes
Cooking time: About 1 hour
Yield: 4 servings

Nutrition information per serving:

Calories	670
Fat	40 g
Cholesterol	225 mg
Sodium	1,325 mg
Carbohydrate	15 g
Protein	63 g

Though every U.S. city probably has at least one Chinese restaurant, real Chinese cuisine remains a mystery to most Americans. The flavors and textures of ingredients such as fermented bean curd and dried fish remain foreign. This duck, a special dish to celebrate the new year, is flavored with soy sauce, dried black mushrooms, pickled cabbage, and ginkgo nuts, available at most Chinese or Asian markets. This recipe is adapted from one by Kail and Alfred Hsu, co-owners of Szechwan East Restaurant in Chicago's Streeterville neighborhood.

1 4½- to 5-pound whole duckling
¼ cup dark soy sauce
3 tablespoons vegetable oil
1 large onion, sliced
3 thin slices peeled gingerroot
Dash salt
5 cups boiling water
1 tablespoon sherry or cognac
1 tablespoon rock sugar or raw sugar
6 dried black mushrooms, soaked in boiling water
   5 minutes, drained and sliced
½ cup ginkgo nuts, rinsed and drained, or water
   chestnuts
1 tablespoon pickled cabbage or lettuce, optional

1. Trim excess fat from duck. Remove and discard giblets. Brush inside and outside of duck with 2 tablespoons soy sauce; set aside to marinate.

2. Heat 1 tablespoon oil in a wok or skillet. Stir-fry onion, ginger, and salt for 2 minutes; remove from heat and set aside.

3. Heat remaining 2 tablespoons oil in the same pan; cook duck over high heat, carefully turning constantly, about 4 minutes.

4. Remove duck to a large, heavy pot. Add remaining 2 tablespoons soy sauce, boiling water, sherry, and rock sugar. Heat to a boil. Reduce heat; cook 15 minutes.

5. Turn duck over in the pot; add mushrooms, ginkgo nuts, onion mixture, and pickled cabbage. Cook 20 minutes or until duck is tender. The duck will still be pink at this point. For more well-done meat, cook an additional 20 minutes or until juices run clear. Remove duck from pan; cook sauce until thickened.

6. Carve duck or cut into large pieces on a cutting board. Arrange the pieces on a serving plate; pour sauce over duck.

Grilled Steak with Spicy Guajillo Sauce

Preparation time: 1 hour

Soaking time: 30 minutes

Marinating time: 30 minutes
to 4 hours

Cooking time: 1¼ hours

Yield: 6 servings

Nutrition information per serving:

Calories	400
Fat	18 g
Cholesterol	115 mg
Sodium	1,345 mg
Carbohydrate	15 g
Protein	44 g

Frontera Grill chef-owner Rick Bayless set out to prove that Mexican cuisine has as much variety and subtlety as any in Europe or Asia. This charcoaled beef "lit up by the shimmering spicy richness of slow-simmered guajillo sauce" is a perfect example, Bayless writes in his cookbook, Mexican Kitchen: Capturing the Vibrant Flavors of a World-Class Cuisine.

Sauce

6 cloves garlic, unpeeled

16 dried guajillo chilies (4 ounces), stemmed and seeded

1 teaspoon dried oregano

¼ teaspoon freshly ground black pepper

⅛ teaspoon ground cumin

3⅔ cups beef broth, plus more if needed

2 tablespoons plus 1½ teaspoons vegetable oil

1½ teaspoons salt

1½ teaspoons sugar

Steaks

1 tablespoon cider vinegar

½ teaspoon salt

6 6-ounce steaks, such as sirloin, tenderloin, or New York strip

1 large red onion, sliced into ½-inch rounds

Cilantro sprigs

1. For the sauce, roast garlic on an ungreased griddle or in a skillet over medium heat until soft, about 15 minutes; cool and peel. Split chilies; toast on griddle 1 or 2 at a time, pressing flat with a spatula until chilies crackle and send up a whiff of smoke, about 20 seconds; flip and toast other side. Soak toasted chilies in a bowl of hot water 30 minutes. Drain; discard water.

2. Puree chilies with oregano, black pepper, cumin, and ⅔ cup broth in a blender or a food processor fitted with a metal blade (add a little more broth if needed). Press through a medium strainer into a bowl. Heat 1 tablespoon plus 1½ teaspoons oil in a heavy, 4-quart saucepan over medium-high heat. Add puree; stir constantly until reduced to a thick paste, 5 to 7 minutes. Reduce heat to medium-low; stir in remaining 3 cups broth. Cover partly; simmer about 45 minutes. Stir in more broth if needed for saucelike consistency. Taste; season with salt and sugar. Remove from heat.

3. For steaks, mix ¼ cup sauce with vinegar and salt in a large bowl. Add steaks; turn to coat. Cover; let stand 30 minutes. (Don't marinate longer than 4 hours, or it will affect the color and texture of the meat.)

4. Prepare grill or broiler. When hot, cook steaks about 8 inches from heat source 4 to 5 minutes per side for medium rare. While steaks are cooking, separate onions into rings and toss with remaining tablespoon of oil. Spread onions on grill around steaks; cook, turning with tongs, until lightly browned, 6 to 8 minutes.

5. Reheat sauce to a simmer; serve with steaks and onions. Garnish with cilantro sprigs.

Pepper Beef

Preparation time: 15 minutes
Marinating time: 30 minutes
Cooking time: 10 minutes
Yield: 4 servings

Chinese food, the world's oldest recorded culinary catechism, is being rediscovered and reinterpreted by health- and convenience-oriented Americans. This is a quick take on a classic Chinese dish, inspired by a recipe from The 15 Minute Chinese Gourmet, *by Elizabeth Chiu King. Serve with steamed rice or cooked noodles.*

Nutrition information per serving:

Calories	400
Fat	30 g
Cholesterol	65 mg
Sodium	1,130 mg
Carbohydrate	10 g
Protein	23 g

2 tablespoons soy sauce
1 tablespoon dry sherry, gin, or vodka, optional
1 teaspoon Asian sesame oil
1 teaspoon sugar
¼ teaspoon ground black pepper
2 8-ounce boneless strip steaks, well trimmed
¾ cup chicken broth
2 tablespoons oyster sauce or Worcestershire sauce
2 teaspoons cornstarch
2 tablespoons vegetable oil
1 large onion, halved and sliced
1 large green bell pepper, seeded and cut into 1-inch-
    square-pieces
¼ teaspoon salt

1. Mix soy sauce, sherry, sesame oil, sugar, and black pepper in a large bowl. Cut steaks into 1-inch-wide strips, then into 1-inch cubes. Add to soy sauce mixture; let marinate 30 minutes.

2. Mix together chicken broth, oyster sauce, and cornstarch in a small bowl. Set aside.

3. Heat a large skillet or wok over high heat 30 seconds. Add 1 tablespoon oil; swirl to coat skillet; let heat 30 seconds. Add onion and bell pepper. Stir-fry 2 minutes. Add salt; mix well. Remove to bowl or platter.

4. Add remaining 1 tablespoon oil to skillet; heat 30 seconds. Add beef cubes, reserving marinade. Stir-fry until meat loses its pink color, 3 to 4 minutes. Add onion and pepper; mix well.

5. Stir in marinade; cook 1 minute. Add chicken broth mixture; stir-fry until liquid thickens, about 1 minute. Transfer to a serving platter.

Spicy Orange Beef

Preparation time: 45 minutes
Freezing time: 1 to 2 hours
Cooking time: 15 minutes
Yield: 4 servings

Scaling down restaurant recipes for home kitchens without losing the essential character of a dish is always tricky. This one, adapted from one served at the former Austin Koo's Restaurant in Chicago's Loop, tenderizes chewy flank steak by slicing it ultrathin. Freezing the beef slightly beforehand eases the cutting.

1 flank steak, about 1½ pounds

Marinade
2 large egg whites
½ cup reduced-sodium soy sauce
¼ cup cornstarch
¼ cup rice wine or dry sherry
12 pieces dried orange peel, available at Asian markets

Nutrition information per serving:

Calories	815
Fat	22 g
Cholesterol	80 mg
Sodium	600 mg
Carbohydrate	90 g
Protein	48 g

For Cooking
1 pound broccoli
1 red bell pepper, seeded
1 green bell pepper, seeded
1¼ cups defatted, low-sodium chicken broth
5 tablespoons rice wine or dry sherry
2 tablespoons sugar
¼ to ½ teaspoon crushed red pepper flakes, to taste
1 tablespoon cornstarch dissolved in 2 tablespoons water
2 tablespoons vegetable oil
3 green onions, minced
1 medium clove garlic, minced
2 teaspoons grated gingerroot
2 tablespoons water
1 8-ounce can bamboo shoots, drained
1 teaspoon Asian sesame oil
6 cups cooked white rice
Chopped cilantro for garnish

1. Freeze flank steak for easier slicing, until almost firm, 1 to 2 hours. Cut flank steak across grain into thin strips using a sharp slicing knife.

2. For the marinade, beat egg whites in a large bowl until frothy. Stir in soy sauce, cornstarch, and wine until smooth. Stir in orange peel; add sliced flank steak; mix well to coat. Marinate 10 minutes.

3. Lightly peel broccoli stalks; slice into ¼-inch-thick slices. Separate florets into bite-sized pieces. Put broccoli into a large pot of boiling water; cook 2 minutes. Drain well.

4. Cut peppers into bite-sized pieces. Mix chicken broth, wine, sugar, and red pepper in a small bowl. Dissolve cornstarch in water in a separate small bowl.

5. Heat a well-seasoned wok or large skillet until hot. Add 1 tablespoon oil; heat to very hot. Add half of the green onions, garlic, and ginger; stir-fry 30 seconds. Add half of the drained steak and orange peel. Stir-fry over high heat until no longer pink, 2 to 3 minutes. Remove from wok with a slotted spoon. Repeat using 1 more tablespoon oil and the remaining green onions, garlic, ginger, and steak. Remove from wok.

6. Add peppers and 2 tablespoons water to the wok; cook, stirring over high heat until crisp-tender, about 2 minutes. Stir in broccoli and bamboo shoots; cook, stirring, 1 minute. Return beef to wok. Stir in broth mixture; heat to a simmer. Stir in dissolved cornstarch; cook, stirring, until thickened. Stir in sesame oil. Serve over rice; garnish with cilantro.

Korean Barbecued Beef Short Ribs

Preparation time: 20 minutes

Marinating time: 2½ hours or
   overnight

Cooking time: 30 minutes

Yield: 8 servings

Nutrition information per
serving:

Calories	415
Fat	28 g
Cholesterol	110 mg
Sodium	455 mg
Carbohydrate	3 g
Protein	37 g

NOTE

Cooking ribs longer and more
slowly by the indirect method
of grilling results in more
tender meat.

*The Korean enthusiasm for grilled meats and barbecued ribs
is something any Midwesterner or Southerner can understand.
The twist at Korean barbecue restaurants is the numerous
accompanying salads and the baskets of red leaf lettuce in
which to wrap the cooked meat.*

2 tablespoons plus 2 teaspoons sesame seeds, toasted in
   a dry skillet
3 cloves garlic, minced
4 green onions, finely chopped
1 inch-long piece gingerroot, minced
¼ cup sake, mirin, dry sherry, or dry vermouth
2 tablespoons Asian sesame oil
3 to 4 pounds beef short ribs
2 tablespoons vegetable oil

1. Combine 2 tablespoons toasted sesame seeds with garlic,
   green onions, ginger, sake, and sesame oil in a small bowl.
   Place ribs in a zip-seal plastic food storage bag; pour marinade over. Squeeze out air; seal. Refrigerate 2½ hours or
   overnight.

2. Prepare grill or broiler. Remove ribs from marinade,
   reserving marinade. Brush ribs with vegetable oil. Grill or
   broil ribs 15 minutes per side, turning once. Spoon reserved
   marinade over ribs every 5 minutes, being sure to allow 5
   minutes of cooking after last application of marinade. Ribs
   should be golden brown. Sprinkle with remaining 2 teaspoons sesame seeds.

Thai-Style Hamburgers

Arun Sampanthavivat, owner of Arun's in Chicago, remodeled the classic grilled burger using the Thai flavors of lemongrass and lime leaves (available at Thai markets). The grated zest of 1 or 2 limes can be substituted.

3 slices white bread
2 pounds lean ground pork
1 large egg, lightly beaten
6 lime leaves, finely minced
½ cup finely minced lemongrass
2 tablespoons chopped cilantro
1 tablespoon tapioca flour or cornstarch
1 tablespoon vegetable oil
1¼ teaspoons soy sauce
1 teaspoon minced garlic
1 teaspoon salt
½ teaspoon freshly ground black pepper
¼ teaspoon white pepper
¼ teaspoon paprika
¼ teaspoon sugar
All-purpose flour
Hamburger buns
Toppings: fresh basil, mint, or cilantro; chili paste;
    mayonnaise; lettuce; tomatoes; cucumber slices; onions

Preparation time: 30 minutes
Cooking time: 10 minutes
Yield: 8 servings

Nutrition information per burger:

Calories	430
Fat	22 g
Cholesterol	105 mg
Sodium	695 mg
Carbohydrate	30 g
Protein	26 g

1. Prepare a grill or broiler. Put bread into a large bowl. Cover with hot water and soak 10 minutes; drain. Squeeze dry; return to the bowl. Mix the bread to a paste. Add the remaining ingredients except flour, buns, and toppings; mix lightly.

2. Shape the mixture into eight patties. Grill or broil the patties 6 inches from the heat source, turning once, until they are no longer pink in the center, 8 to 10 minutes. Serve on buns with toppings of your choice.

Vietnamese-Style Noodles in Spicy Broth

Preparation time: 45 minutes

Cooking time: 30 minutes

Yield: 6 servings

Nutrition information per serving:

Calories	255
Fat	6 g
Cholesterol	25 mg
Sodium	1,080 mg
Carbohydrate	34 g
Protein	16 g

The Vietnamese make extensive use of dried, packaged rice noodles, bahn pho, often called "rice sticks." Before cooking them, soak them for 20 to 30 minutes.

½ pound boneless beef sirloin or skinless chicken breast, thinly sliced

1 to 2 tablespoons fish sauce (*nam pla*)

½ to 1 teaspoon crushed red pepper flakes

½ teaspoon sugar

¼ teaspoon freshly ground black pepper

12 ounces dried rice noodles (*bahn pho*)

2 13¾-ounce cans beef broth

2 13¾-ounce cans reduced-sodium chicken broth

2 stalks fresh lemongrass, thinly sliced

1 1½-piece gingerroot, lightly crushed

1 tablespoon oil

1 onion, halved and sliced

2 cloves garlic, minced

2 large carrots, thinly sliced

1 chayote squash, peeled, seeded, and cubed, or 2 medium zucchini, halved and thickly sliced

1 cup shredded spinach or other dark greens

1 lime, cut into wedges

3 green onions, thinly sliced

12 to 16 sprigs fresh mint

12 to 16 sprigs cilantro

Hot sauce or minced fresh chilies to taste

1. Mix sliced beef or chicken with fish sauce, pepper flakes, sugar, and black pepper in a small bowl. Let stand about 20 minutes. Put noodles into a large bowl; add very hot water to cover; let stand until softened, about 20 minutes; drain well.

2. Put broth, lemongrass, and ginger into a large dutch oven or soup pot. Simmer 20 minutes.

3. Heat a wok or large skillet; add oil. Add onion; stir-fry until golden, about 5 minutes; add garlic and meat mixture. Stir-fry until meat is no longer pink, 2 to 4 minutes. Remove from heat.

4. Strain lemongrass and ginger from broth; return broth to pot. Add carrots; simmer 5 minutes. Add chayote; simmer 5 minutes. Add meat mixture, drained noodles, and shredded greens; simmer until greens wilt, about 5 minutes. Taste and adjust seasonings.

5. Put lime wedges, green onions, mint, cilantro, and hot sauce into small bowls to pass at the table for garnishes. Pour soup into bowls; serve.

Belgian Meatballs Braised in Beer

Preparation time: 35 minutes
Cooking time: 1 hour
Yield: 6 servings

Nutrition information per serving:

Calories	330
Fat	20 g
Cholesterol	115 mg
Sodium	185 mg
Carbohydrate	12 g
Protein	25 g

Belgians produce more than 300 types of beer, some of them flavored with fruit, berries, and mixtures of spices. These meatballs, though, require a relatively tame pilsener. Choose a full-bodied variety rather than a mainstream American beer. This recipe is adapted from Everybody Eats Well in Belgium Cookbook, *by Ruth Van Waerebeek.*

Meatballs
1 cup fresh white bread crumbs
⅓ cup milk
1 pound lean ground beef
½ pound ground pork or veal
1 large egg
1 tablespoon finely minced shallots
1 tablespoon finely minced fresh parsley
½ teaspoon salt
Freshly ground pepper to taste
Pinch freshly grated nutmeg
2 tablespoons all-purpose flour
2 tablespoons unsalted butter
1 tablespoon vegetable oil

Sauce
1 medium onion, thinly sliced
2 Belgian endives, cored and cut into ¼-inch slices
1 teaspoon sugar
Salt to taste
Freshly ground pepper to taste
2 tablespoons all-purpose flour
1 cup pilsener-style beer
½ cup chicken or beef broth
2 tablespoons finely minced fresh parsley, for garnish

1. For meatballs, soak bread crumbs in milk in a small bowl until thoroughly moistened; squeeze dry with hands. Combine bread crumbs, ground meats, egg, shallots, parsley, salt, pepper, and nutmeg in a medium bowl. Form mixture into 6 to 8 balls or patties (2 inches in diameter and ½ inch thick); dust with flour.

2. Heat butter and oil in a deep, heavy dutch oven until hot but not smoking, over high heat. Add meatballs; cook until browned on all sides, about 5 minutes, making sure butter does not burn. Remove meatballs to platter; keep warm.

3. To prepare the sauce, discard all but 2 tablespoons of the fat in the pan. Add onion and endives. Cook over low heat, stirring constantly, about 10 minutes. Add sugar, salt, pepper, and flour to vegetables; cook, stirring, 1 to 2 minutes. Add beer and broth; heat to a quick boil, scraping up brown bits from bottom of pan.

4. Reduce heat to a simmer; return meatballs to pan, placing on top of vegetables. Simmer, partly covered, until meat is cooked through, about 45 minutes. Sprinkle with parsley.

Deli-Style Cabbage Rolls with Rice and Meat

Preparation time: 1 hour

Cooking time: 1 hour

Yield: 8 servings, about 16
   rolls

Nutrition information per
serving:

Calories	260
Fat	10 g
Cholesterol	65 mg
Sodium	1,060 mg
Carbohydrate	29 g
Protein	18 g

These traditional Polish-style stuffed cabbage rolls are topped with a light tomato sauce and baked on a bed of crisp, fresh sauerkraut. Some cooks have found that freezing the head of cabbage makes it pliable enough to roll. If you'd like to try it, you can skip the blanching in step 1.

1 head cabbage, about 3 pounds
2 slices bacon
1 large onion, finely chopped
2 cloves garlic, minced
1 pound ground meat, combination of ground beef
   round, lean pork, and veal (or chicken)
¼ cup rice, cooked
1 egg, lightly beaten
1½ tablespoons sweet paprika, preferably Hungarian
½ teaspoon marjoram
1 teaspoon salt
Freshly ground black pepper to taste
2 pounds fresh sauerkraut
½ teaspoon caraway seeds
2 cups crushed tomatoes with added puree
½ cup beef or chicken broth
Chopped fresh parsley for garnish

1. Heat water in a large pot to a boil. Core cabbage; remove wilted outer leaves, setting them aside for later use. Skewer cabbage through core with a large fork; place in boiling water to cover; cook 2 minutes. Lift out cabbage. Remove softened outer leaves; set leaves aside. Repeat until you have 16 leaves for stuffing; reserve remaining cabbage.

2. For the filling, cook bacon in a large skillet until crisp. Drain; reserving fat. Set bacon aside. Return 1 tablespoon bacon fat to the pan. Add onion and garlic; cook, stirring, until softened. Transfer to a mixing bowl. Stir in ground meats, cooked rice, egg, paprika, marjoram, salt, and pepper. Mix well.

3. Heat oven to 350°F. Rinse sauerkraut under cold running water; drain well. Heat reserved bacon fat in the same skillet. Add sauerkraut, caraway seeds, and pepper to taste. Cook, stirring, until softened and lightly coated with bacon fat, about 2 minutes. Spread over the bottom of a 9″ × 13″ baking pan. Sprinkle with crisp bacon.

4. To stuff the cabbage leaves, trim away the thick center vein from the bottom of each large leaf. Shape ¼ cup filling into a log; place in the center of a leaf perpendicular to the stem. Fold the sides of the leaf over the filling; roll up, starting at stem end. Repeat with remaining leaves.

5. Arrange cabbage rolls on top of sauerkraut. Mix tomatoes with broth; pour over cabbage rolls. Cover rolls with a layer of unused cabbage leaves. Bake, covered, until the cabbage rolls are cooked through and the sauce is bubbly, about 1 hour. Discard the top layer of cabbage leaves. Garnish with parsley.

Chicago-Style Deep-Dish Pizza

Preparation time: 1 hour
Cooking time: 1 hour
Yield: 6 servings

Nutritional information per serving:

Calories	735
Fat	35 g
Cholesterol	60 mg
Sodium	1,255 mg
Carbohydrates	71 g
Protein	34 g

Though not an authentic Italian dish, deep-dish pizza is Chicago's own. This is the recipe that the Chicago Tribune test kitchen developed to try to duplicate the version found at Gino's East Pizzeria in Streeterville. If you like a lot of crunch in your crust, sprinkle additional cornmeal in the pan before adding the dough.

Crust

1 cup water
¼ cup vegetable shortening
¼ teaspoon salt
1 package (¼ ounce) active dry yeast
½ cup warm water (105°F to 115°F)
¾ cup yellow cornmeal
3 to 3½ cups all-purpose flour

Filling

1 can (28 ounces) Italian-style plum tomatoes
2 teaspoons vegetable oil
1 small onion, chopped
1 green bell pepper, chopped
1 clove garlic, minced
¾ teaspoon dried oregano
½ teaspoon fennel seeds
½ teaspoon salt
¼ teaspoon freshly ground black pepper
¼ pound fresh mushrooms, sliced
1 pound mild Italian sausage, cooked and crumbled
1 package (10 ounces) mozzarella cheese, thinly sliced
½ cup freshly grated Parmesan cheese

1. Heat oven to 425°F. For crust, heat water, shortening, and salt in small saucepan over medium heat until shortening melts; cool to lukewarm, 105°F to 115°F. Dissolve yeast in ½ cup warm water; let stand until bubbly. Mix yeast and shortening mixtures in large bowl; stir in cornmeal. Add 2 cups flour; beat well. Stir in enough additional flour to make soft dough. Turn onto lightly floured surface; knead, working in more flour as needed, until smooth and elastic. Press dough evenly over bottom and up sides of greased 12-inch round, 2-inch deep pizza pan. Bake 5 minutes.

2. For filling, chop tomatoes and drain in colander; set aside. Heat oil in medium saucepan over medium heat. Add onion, green pepper, garlic, oregano, fennel seeds, salt, and pepper; cook until onion and green pepper are tender, about 4 minutes. Stir in drained tomatoes and mushrooms; cook 2 minutes. Remove from heat; drain well.

3. Crumble sausage onto pizza crust. Arrange mozzarella slices over sausage. Top with tomato mixture; sprinkle with Parmesan. Bake until crust is golden brown, about 45 minutes. Let stand 5 minutes before serving.

Lasagna with Meat Ragu

Preparation time: 65 minutes

Cooking time: About 3 hours
25 minutes to 4 hours

Standing time: 10 minutes

Yield: 10 servings

Nutrition information per serving:

Calories	675
Fat	36 g
Cholesterol	120 mg
Sodium	1,085 mg
Carbohydrate	49 g
Protein	42 g

There are multitudes of lasagnas in the Italian lexicon. This recipe is a version developed in the Chicago Tribune *Test Kitchen, using ingredients from several regions and inspiration from cookbook authors Nancy Verde Barr and Carlos Middione. The ragu is similar to sauces made in Naples, hearty mixtures that have large cuts of several types of meat simmered in the sauce and removed before serving. The meat traditionally is used in another meal, but here we return it to the ragu.*

Ragu

3 tablespoons olive oil

½ pound eye of round beef (in one piece)

½ pound pork short ribs

1 piece veal shank, about 8 ounces

1 onion, diced

1 small carrot, minced

1 celery rib, minced

3 28-ounce cans crushed tomatoes, partly drained

1 6-ounce can tomato paste

10 fresh basil leaves, chopped

Salt to taste

Freshly ground pepper to taste

Lasagna

1 12-ounce box lasagna noodles

2 tablespoons olive oil

½ pound mild or hot Italian sausage, casing removed, finely crumbled

½ cup chopped fresh basil

3 tablespoons chopped fresh oregano

Salt to taste

Freshly ground pepper to taste

1 pound (16 ounces) ricotta cheese, preferably whole-milk

1 large egg, lightly beaten
4 cups (16 ounces) shredded mozzarella cheese
1 cup (4 ounces) grated Parmesan cheese

1. For the ragu, heat oil in a large pot over medium-high heat. Pat meats dry; brown on all sides, about 10 minutes. Add onion, carrot, and celery. Cook until softened, 5 minutes. Add tomatoes, tomato paste, basil, salt, and pepper. Heat to a boil; cook 15 minutes. Lower heat; simmer, partly covered, until meats are tender and falling off bone, about 2 to 2½ hours. Stir occasionally, adding water if sauce gets too thick. Remove meats from sauce; pull meat from bones and shred. Return to sauce. Adjust seasoning. (Can be made a day ahead and refrigerated.)

2. Cook lasagna noodles in boiling water according to package directions. Drain; arrange noodles on a clean towel. Heat oil in a medium skillet. Add sausage; cook until browned. Drain. Add basil, oregano, salt, and pepper; set aside. Stir ricotta cheese and egg together in a small bowl; set aside.

3. Heat oven to 375°F. Oil a 9″ × 13″ baking pan. Fill bottom of pan with a layer of lasagna noodles, overlapping slightly. Cover with layers of ragu and sausage mixture. Dot the surface with large spoonfuls of ricotta, spreading slightly. Sprinkle with cheeses. Add more noodles; layer again until all ingredients are used. Top layers should be ragu, mozzarella, and Parmesan. Bake until bubbly and heated through, 55 to 70 minutes. Let stand 10 minutes before slicing.

Glazed Irish Bacon (or Corned Beef) with Vegetables

Preparation time: 40 minutes

Cooking time: About 4 hours

Yield: 8 servings

Nutrition information per serving (using corned beef):

Calories	870
Fat	44 g
Cholesterol	220 mg
Sodium	2,650 mg
Carbohydrate	72 g
Protein	49 g

Immigrants often have to improvise, in the kitchen and elsewhere, when they attempt to duplicate a bit of back home. A standard pork dish became corned beef and cabbage for many Irish when they came over. But for Chicago's Irish-Americans, a surprising number of Irish food imports make their way to the States, ensuring that they can authentically satisfy certain cravings—hearty oats from County Waterford, cured pork loin bacon from County Kildare, Irish tea blended in Galway to suit the Irish taste, honey from County Kilkenny, and a even bit of Blarney cheese.

1 piece Irish boiling bacon or 1 corned beef, about
　4 pounds

2 bay leaves

8 peppercorns

2 whole allspice

1 small cinnamon stick

1 teaspoon mustard seeds

Glaze

½ cup packed dark-brown sugar

1½ teaspoons dry mustard powder

2 tablespoons light molasses

2 tablespoons Irish whiskey, bourbon, or water

Vegetables

12 to 16 small red potatoes, peeled if desired

8 thin carrots, with ½ inch of green tops, peeled

1 pint small brussels sprouts, cored, optional

8 white radishes, peeled, optional

12 large green onions, trimmed

1 large head savoy or green cabbage, cut into 8 wedges

1. Place bacon or corned beef in a 6-quart pot or dutch oven. Add bay leaves and spices; add cold water to cover by 2 inches. Heat to a boil over medium heat; reduce heat to a simmer. Cover; simmer until fork-tender, allowing 45 to 60 minutes per pound.

2. Meanwhile, mix all glaze ingredients in a small bowl; prepare vegetables.

3. Heat oven to 375°F. Remove meat to a large baking pan; reserve cooking liquid. Coat the top of the meat thoroughly with some of the glaze. Carefully pour 2 cups meat-cooking liquid into the baking pan. Bake meat, uncovered, reapplying glaze as desired, until top is nicely browned, about 15 minutes.

4. Reheat meat-cooking liquid to a boil; reduce heat to a simmer. Add potatoes and carrots; cover. Cook 10 minutes. Add brussels sprouts and radishes, if using; cook, uncovered, 10 minutes. Add green onions and cabbage wedges; cook, uncovered, until all vegetables are tender but not soft, about 10 minutes more.

5. Thinly slice meat; arrange on a serving platter. Drain vegetables; arrange around meat. Drizzle some of the baking pan juices over all.

Barbecued Roast Pork

Preparation time: 25 minutes

Marinating time: 6 hours

Cooking time: 45 minutes

Yield: 4 servings

This pork entree was adapted from a Chinese restaurant recipe so that home cooks could find most of the ingredients in conventional supermarkets. Instead of marinating the roast in a pan, you can as easily do the job in a zip-seal plastic bag. Squeeze out the excess air so the marinade surrounds the entire roast. Serve this with stir-fried vegetables.

Nutrition information per serving:

Calories	635
Fat	10 g
Cholesterol	100 mg
Sodium	595 mg
Carbohydrate	85 g
Protein	46 g

3 green onions, cut into 2-inch lengths

1 1½-inch slice gingerroot, finely chopped

3 tablespoons sugar

3 tablespoons ketchup

2 tablespoons hoisin sauce

2 tablespoons reduced-sodium soy sauce

2 tablespoons dry sherry

2 cloves garlic, minced

1 drop red food color, optional

1 boneless pork loin roast, trimmed, about 1½ pounds

6 cups cooked white rice

1. Put onions, ginger, sugar, ketchup, hoisin sauce, soy sauce, sherry, garlic, and food color into a shallow nonaluminum container. Mix well. Add pork roast; turn to coat. Cover; refrigerate 6 hours, turning roast occasionally.

2. Heat oven to 350°F. Remove roast from marinade; put roast on a rack set in a roasting pan. Roast, basting occasionally with marinade, until the internal temperature registers 160°F on a meat or instant-read thermometer, about 45 minutes.

3. Heat any remaining marinade in a small saucepan to a hard boil. Slice meat thinly; serve with rice and some of the boiled marinade.

Swedish Baked Ham

The Swedish Christmas smorgasbord includes an enormous array of foods: herring, pâtés, head cheese, Goteborg sausage, scalloped potatoes, limpa bread, large circles of knackenbrod (Swedish hardtack), Swedish meatballs, smoked salmon, smoked eel, red and brown cabbages, and a bowl of rice porridge containing a single almond. At the center of all this bounty is often a large fresh ham.

1 whole smoked fresh ham, about 12 pounds, see Note
3 tablespoons whole-grain mustard, Swedish or Dijon
1 tablespoon Swedish light syrup or honey
1 tablespoon potato starch or cornstarch
1 large egg yolk
Fine dry bread crumbs

1. Heat oven to 250°F. Put ham into a shallow roasting pan; cover tightly with foil. Put meat thermometer into the ham without touching the bone. Bake until the thermometer registers 160°F, about 30 minutes per pound. Remove from oven; cool. Trim off skin and fat. (Recipe can be prepared to this point up to two days in advance; refrigerate covered.)

2. Heat oven to 400°F. Mix mustard, syrup, potato starch, and egg yolk in a small bowl. Spread over ham. Sprinkle generously with bread crumbs. Bake until ham is heated through and crumbs are golden, about 45 minutes.

Preparation time: 25 minutes
Cooking time: About 7 hours
Yield: 15 servings

Nutrition information per serving:

Calories	545
Fat	36 g
Cholesterol	145 mg
Sodium	2,590 mg
Carbohydrate	7 g
Protein	46 g

NOTE

You may substitute a fully cooked ham if desired. A fully cooked ham only needs to be cooked to an internal temperature of 140°F, about 20 minutes a pound.

Roast Lamb with Garlic, Herbs, and Wild Mushrooms

Preparation time: 30 minutes
Cooking time: 1¾ to 2 hours
Yield: 10 servings

Nutrition information per serving:

Calories	420
Fat	20 g
Cholesterol	150 mg
Sodium	820 mg
Carbohydrate	9 g
Protein	50 g

A 1991 benefit home tour in the Beverly neighborhood on Chicago's Southwest Side was the occasion for a French country Christmas feast prepared by chef-caterer James Boardman. "It's the time of year when you want an assortment of food, filling food, not light things," he said. "It should look rich and colorful." This lamb could be the centerpiece for such a holiday feast.

¼ cup fresh sage sprigs
¼ cup fresh rosemary sprigs
¼ cup fresh thyme sprigs
3 to 4 large cloves garlic, peeled
2 large shallots, peeled
¼ cup plus 2 tablespoons olive oil
2 tablespoons red-wine vinegar
1 tablespoon celery seed
1 tablespoon salt
2 teaspoons cracked black pepper
1 large leg of lamb, about 5 pounds, boned, rolled, and tied
2 tablespoons unsalted butter
3 pounds mushrooms, preferably a mix of wild and domestic, wiped clean

1. Heat oven to 350°F. Mince herb sprigs, garlic, and shallots in a blender or a food processor fitted with a metal blade. Add ¼ cup oil and the vinegar, celery seed, salt, and pepper; mix to a paste. Spread over lamb; place in a shallow roasting pan.

2. Roast lamb about 20 to 25 minutes a pound or until meat thermometer reads 140°F for rare, 145 to 150°F for medium-rare.

3. Shortly before lamb is fully cooked, heat remaining 2 tablespoons oil and the butter over high heat in a large skillet. Add mushrooms and salt and pepper to taste. Cook until soft, about 10 minutes. Carve lamb into thin slices; overlap on a large platter. Surround with mushrooms.

Lamb Shanks with Onions, Tomatoes, and Peppers

Preparation time: 40 minutes

Cooking time: 2 hours

Yield: 6 servings

Hungary, blessed with Central Europe's most intriguing cuisine, has a taste for stews, sour cream, and meat grilled over outdoor fires. The Turks introduced coffee and quite possibly paprika, the national spice. Onions also are primal in many dishes, including this one.

Nutrition information per serving:

Calories	375
Fat	18 g
Cholesterol	95 mg
Sodium	110 mg
Carbohydrate	27 g
Protein	30 g

Lamb

1½ pounds pork bones

6 lamb shanks, 12 to 14 ounces each

2 tablespoons pickling spice

3 large ribs celery, diced

3 large carrots, diced

1 yellow banana pepper, diced

4 cloves garlic, minced

Vegetables

2 tablespoons vegetable oil

1¼ pounds Spanish onions, chopped

3 tablespoons sweet paprika, Hungarian preferred

2 medium tomatoes, seeded and diced

3 medium green bell peppers, seeded and chopped

2 yellow banana peppers, chopped

6 cloves garlic, minced

Salt to taste

1. Heat oven to 350°F. For the lamb, arrange pork bones in a single layer in the bottom of a roasting pan. Top with lamb shanks. Mix together pickling spice, celery, carrots, banana pepper, and garlic in a bowl; scatter over shanks. Pour water into the pan to cover the pork bones and slightly less than half the shanks. Cover; bake until lamb is nearly falling off the bone, about 1½ hours.

2. For the vegetables, about 25 minutes before lamb is done, heat oil in a large skillet. Add onions; cook until soft and golden, about 15 minutes. Stir in paprika; cook 3 minutes. Add tomatoes, bell peppers, banana peppers, garlic, and salt to taste. Cover the skillet; cook until vegetables are barely soft, 5 to 7 minutes. Set aside.

3. Spoon vegetables onto six dinner plates. Top each with a lamb shank. Skim fat off pan juices. Season pan juices to taste; spoon over each shank.

Marinated Lamb Kebabs

Preparation time: 25 minutes

Marinating time: 6 to 8 hours

Cooking time: 12 to 17
   minutes

Yield: 8 servings

Nutrition information per serving:

Calories	220
Fat	10 g
Cholesterol	90 mg
Sodium	70 mg
Carbohydrate	2 g
Protein	29 g

Behind every ethnic storefront restaurant in Chicago lies a tale of immigration and adaptation. Mohammed Al-Ourani started his culinary training as a teenager in Amman, Jordan, where he spent a career as a cook. Later he came to Chicago to join his son, and Al-Ourani ended up starting his own restaurant, Jerusalem, in the Marquette Park neighborhood. This recipe is popular there. The traditional accompaniment is rice pilaf garnished with toasted almonds and pine nuts.

1 pound onions, cut in chunks

2 cloves garlic, peeled

2 jalapeño chilies, stemmed

⅓ cup olive oil

3 tablespoons fresh lemon juice

Salt to taste

2 teaspoons freshly ground black pepper

2½ pounds lean, cubed lamb, such as leg or shoulder

Cherry tomatoes, optional

Red or green bell peppers, optional

Vidalia onion wedges, optional

1. Puree onions, garlic, and chilies in a food processor fitted with a metal blade. Strain through a fine-meshed strainer. Transfer to a large bowl; stir in oil, lemon juice, salt, and pepper. Add meat, stirring well. Cover; refrigerate 6 to 8 hours.

2. Prepare a medium-hot charcoal fire or place broiler rack 8 inches from heat; heat broiler. Remove lamb from the marinade; thread on 8 skewers. If using vegetables, thread on separate skewers. Grill or broil, turning once, until meat is cooked as desired and vegetables are crisp-tender, 12 to 17 minutes.

Spaghetti with Butter and Cheese

Italians like cheese more than we do—or at least they eat more of it. According to the Italian Trade Commission, annual per capita consumption is about 35½ pounds in Italy, compared to 28 pounds in the United States. Parmigiano-Reggiano, a superb grating cheese, is sold in huge cylinders and usually aged about three years. In Italy, paper-thin shavings often are served on salads. Pecorino Romano is the most famous of Italy's sheep's-milk cheeses. Hard and grainy with a pleasantly sharp taste, this is a table and grating cheese. This simple recipe is adapted from one by Marcella Hazan, who insists that the secret to its success is the order in which the ingredients are added to the pasta. The other secret, of course, is to use the best ingredients possible.

Preparation time: 20 minutes
Cooking time: 10 minutes
Yield: 6 servings

Nutrition information per serving:

Calories	455
Fat	15 g
Cholesterol	40 mg
Sodium	365 mg
Carbohydrate	60 g
Protein	19 g

1 16-ounce package spaghetti
1 cup freshly grated Parmesan cheese
3 tablespoons unsalted butter, softened
2 tablespoons whipping cream
Salt to taste
Freshly ground pepper to taste
¼ cup freshly grated pecorino Romano cheese

1. Put a sturdy ceramic pasta bowl in an oven set to its lowest setting, about 170°F. Cook spaghetti in a large pot of boiling salted water according to package directions. Drain well; transfer to the heated bowl.

2. Immediately add ½ cup Parmesan; toss until cheese melts. Add butter; toss until melted. Add cream, remaining ½ cup Parmesan, salt, and pepper. Toss six to eight times. Sprinkle pecorino Romano and additional pepper over the top.

Gnocchi with Mushroom Broth

Preparation time: 40 minutes

Cooking time: 20 minutes

Yield: 4 servings

Nutrition information per serving:

Calories	355
Fat	22 g
Cholesterol	55 mg
Sodium	690 mg
Carbohydrate	29 g
Protein	13 g

Gnocchi (NUO-key) are small, northern Italian dumplings made with potatoes and flour. The tender nuggets are served like pasta and are well suited to light sauces and delicate flavorings. Some markets offer fresh gnocchi, but the frozen ones, more commonly available, are convenient and impressive. If you can't find them, try using orrichetti or pasta shells. An indulgent hand might add some of the wild varieties of mushrooms, but even button mushrooms result in a flavorful, easy main course.

1 pound fresh or frozen gnocchi

3 tablespoons unsalted butter

1 large clove garlic, minced

¼ cup oil-packed sun-dried tomatoes, patted dry and finely chopped

1 small red bell pepper, diced

1 tablespoon minced fresh rosemary

1 pound mushrooms, a mix of several kinds, halved

Salt to taste

Freshly ground peppper to taste

Nutmeg to taste

1 cup reduced-sodium chicken broth

1 cup beef broth

½ cup grated Parmesan cheese

1. Cook the gnocchi according to package instructions or until they rise to the top of the water. Drain; set aside.

2. Melt butter in a 12-inch skillet. Add garlic; cook gently until fragrant, about 2 minutes. Add sun-dried tomatoes, bell pepper, and rosemary. Cook, stirring often, until pepper begins to soften, about 3 minutes.

3. Increase the heat to high; add mushrooms. Add salt, pepper, and nutmeg to taste. Cook, stirring often, until mushrooms begin to soften, about 3 to 4 minutes. Add the chicken broth and beef broth; heat to simmer. Cook until reduced slightly, 4 to 5 minutes. Stir in the gnocchi. Heat through. Adjust seasonings. Serve in pasta bowls; top with grated cheese.

Vegetarian Pasta with Two Chinese Sauces

Preparation time: 1 hour
Cooking time: 10 minutes
Yield: 16 servings

Nutrition information per serving:

Calories	325
Fat	9 g
Cholesterol	0 mg
Sodium	485 mg
Carbohydrate	52 g
Protein	10 g

NOTE

These ingredients may be purchased at Asian markets. Balsamic vinegar may be substituted for black vinegar. To roast peppercorns, place them in a small skillet over medium heat; cook, shaking pan occasionally, until pepper is aromatic and color barely changes, about 2 minutes. Cool; finely grind in an electric spice grinder or with a mortar and pestle.

Plain spaghetti is the foundation of this example of "East meets West" cuisine. The two traditional Chinese sauces have distinctive flavors and offer a strong contrast when served separately on the same plate. The presentation of the finished dish also is beautiful and appetizing. This recipe by Dapeng Ren won first place in a Chicago Tribune *potluck contest.*

2 pounds spaghetti
2 tablespoons Asian sesame oil

Peanut Sauce
¼ cup olive oil
3 tablespoons creamy peanut butter
3 tablespoons light soy sauce
3 tablespoons Sanxi black vinegar, see Note
2 tablespoons Japanese miso paste, see Note
1 small clove garlic, minced

Szechwan Red Chili Sauce
3 tablespoons soy sauce
2 tablespoons Sanxi black vinegar
2 tablespoons minced gingerroot
2 tablespoons minced green onion
1 tablespoon minced garlic
1 tablespoon sugar
1 tablespoon red chili oil, see Note
1 teaspoon Szechwan peppercorns, roasted, ground, see note

Topping
½ pound fresh mung bean sprouts
2 cucumbers, seeded and shredded
2 carrots, peeled and cut into matchsticks
2 red bell peppers, cut into matchsticks

Glazed Irish Bacon (or Corned Beef) with Vegetables, page 130

Spaghetti with Butter and Cheese, page 139

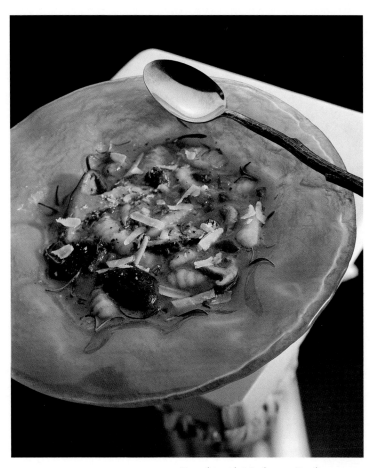

Gnocchi with Mushroom Broth, page 140

Roasted Asparagus with Proscuitto and Basil Viniagrette, page 148

Corn Curry, page 152

Braided Easter Bread, page 178

Tiramisu, page 200

Panna Cotta with Caramel Sauce, page 204

4 large mushrooms, cut into strips or thinly sliced
1 cup cilantro, chopped

1. Cook spaghetti according to package directions. Drain well; transfer to a large bowl. Toss with sesame oil. Set aside.

2. For the peanut sauce, blend olive oil with peanut butter in a small bowl; stir in remaining peanut sauce ingredients. Set aside.

3. For the Szechwan sauce, mix all sauce ingredients in a small bowl. Set aside.

4. Cook bean sprouts in boiling water 15 seconds. Rinse with cold water; drain. Toss pasta with vegetables; divide in half. Place half in another bowl. Toss half with peanut sauce and the other half with Szechwan sauce. Serve on opposite ends of a platter. Sprinkle cilantro over all.

Ethiopian Vegetable Stew

Preparation time: 35 minutes
Cooking time: 25 minutes
Yield: 4 servings

Nutrition information per serving:

Calories	210
Fat	6 g
Cholesterol	0 mg
Sodium	500 mg
Carbohydrate	35 g
Protein	4 g

Simple dishes of rice, beans, and vegetables are common in other cultures. They contain more fiber, less meat, and less fat than most American fare. Alecha *is the common name for such a stew from Ethiopia. Alechas normally are served with Ethiopian flat bread, but this one may be served with rice. It's adapted from* Extending the Table: A World Community Cookbook, *by Joetta Handrich Schlabach.*

2 tablespoons vegetable oil
1 clove garlic, minced
1 onion, chopped
1 cup water
3 medium potatoes, chopped in large pieces
2 to 3 carrots, chopped
¾ teaspoon salt
½ teaspoon ground ginger
½ teaspoon ground turmeric
¼ teaspoon black pepper
1 pound cabbage, chopped (about 5 cups)
1 small hot green chili, seeded and quartered, or to taste

1. Heat oil in a large saucepan over medium heat. Add garlic and onion; cook until soft but not brown, about 5 minutes. Add ½ cup water and the potatoes, carrots, ½ teaspoon salt, ginger, turmeric, and black pepper. Cook, stirring, until potatoes and carrots begin to soften, about 10 minutes.

2. Add cabbage, chili, remaining ½ cup water, and remaining ¼ teaspoon salt. Cook, stirring gently to combine and taking care not to mash vegetables, until vegetables are tender, about 10 minutes.

Side Dishes

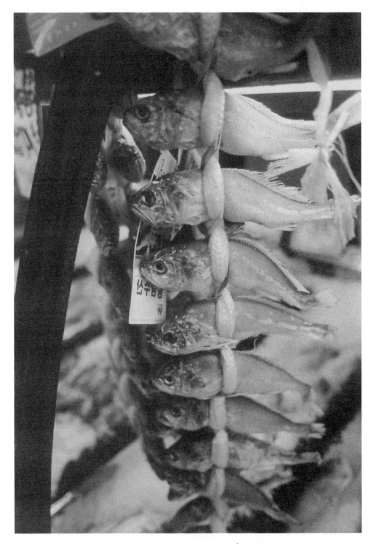

Korean Market, West Lawrence Avenue

Artichokes with Lemon and Dill

Preparation time: 1 hour
Cooking time: 40 minutes
Yield: About 6 servings

Nutrition information per serving :

Calories	150
Fat	7 g
Cholesterol	0 mg
Sodium	655 mg
Carbohydrate	21 g
Protein	5 g

A visit to the Georgulas family in Athens enabled Chicago Tribune *food and wine columnist William Rice to cook a favorite Greek vegetable combination, fresh artichokes stewed in a sweet-sour broth flavored with dill.*

6 tablespoons fresh lemon juice
6 large fresh artichokes
1 lemon, halved
3 tablespoons olive oil
8 green onions, chopped
3 cups water
⅓ cup chopped fresh dill
2 teaspoons sugar
1½ teaspoons salt
2 tablespoons flour
Salt to taste
Pepper to taste

1. Pour 2 tablespoons lemon juice into a large bowl of water. For each artichoke, trim stem; pull off and discard 3 outer bottom layers of leaves, exposing pale green base. Cut off top third of artichoke; discard. Cut artichoke in half through stem. Using a small spoon, remove choke and prickly leaves from center. Rub cut edges of artichokes with cut side of lemon half. Place artichokes in lemon water.

2. Heat oil in a large dutch oven over medium-high heat. Add green onions; cook, stirring, until tender, about 3 minutes. Add water, dill, sugar, salt, and remaining 4 tablespoons lemon juice. Heat to a simmer.

3. Drain artichokes; add to dutch oven. Cover; simmer, occasionally pushing artichokes underwater, until artichoke bottoms are pierced easily with a fork, about 30 minutes. Using a slotted spoon, transfer artichokes to a platter; reserve cooking liquid. Cover artichokes with foil to keep warm.

4. Place flour in a small bowl. Whisk in ½ cup cooking liquid until smooth. Whisk flour mixture into remaining cooking liquid; heat to a boil, whisking constantly. Cook until sauce thickens, stirring constantly, thinning with more water if necessary, about 2 minutes. Season with salt and pepper. Pour over artichokes.

Roasted Asparagus with Prosciutto and Basil Vinaigrette

Preparation time: 20 minutes
Cooking time: 10 minutes
Yield: 6 servings

Nutrition information per serving:

Calories	115
Fat	8 g
Cholesterol	4 mg
Sodium	240 mg
Carbohydrate	9 g
Protein	6 g

This recipe, developed in the Chicago Tribune *Test Kitchen, is an Italian approach to maximizing the freshness of spring asparagus. It's roasted, then tossed in a complementary blanket of prosciutto and a warm dressing featuring fresh basil.*

2 bunches thin asparagus, ends trimmed
3 tablespoons olive oil
¼ teaspoon salt
4 slices (2 ounces total) prosciutto or baked ham, finely diced
2 shallots, minced
3 tablespoons balsamic or red-wine vinegar
1 teaspoon sugar
½ teaspoon Dijon mustard
Freshly ground black pepper to taste
2 to 3 tablespoons finely shredded fresh basil leaves

1. Position oven rack in upper third of oven. Heat oven to 500°F.

2. Put asparagus in a single layer on a large, heavy baking sheet with sides, such as a jelly-roll pan. Add 1 tablespoon oil; toss to coat asparagus. Sprinkle with ⅛ teaspoon salt. Roast, shaking pan once or twice to move asparagus around, until crisp-tender, about 10 minutes.

3. Cook prosciutto and shallots in a medium skillet until slightly golden, about 3 minutes. Stir in remaining 2 table-spoons oil and the vinegar, sugar, and mustard. Heat until sugar dissolves; season with remaining ⅛ teaspoon salt and pepper to taste.

4. Arrange cooked asparagus on a serving platter. Stir basil leaves into vinaigrette mixture; pour over asparagus.

Green Beans with Red and Green Relish

We were thrilled to find bags of trimmed fresh green beans in the supermarket produce aisle. Although trimming a pound of beans takes only a few minutes, there are times when even that is too long. Not wanting to squander the time saved, Chicago Tribune "Fast Food" columnist Pat Dailey looked to Mexico for ingredients such as hot chili, cilantro, and tomatillos, to give the beans a lot of flavor fast. Tomatillos are small green fruit with papery husks that need to be removed before cooking.

1 14½-ounce bag trimmed fresh green beans
1 tablespoon olive oil
1 large shallot, minced
1 teaspoon minced hot chili, or to taste
3 tomatillos, husk removed, cored and chopped
¼ teaspoon salt or to taste
Freshly ground pepper to taste
6 cocktail or cherry tomatoes, chopped
¼ cup minced cilantro

1. Cook beans in boiling water until crisp-tender, 5 to 7 minutes. Drain well; set aside in a serving bowl.

2. Heat oil in the same pan over medium-high heat. Add shallot and hot chili; cook, stirring constantly, until shallot begins to soften, 1 minute. Add tomatillos, salt, and pepper. Cook, stirring, 3 minutes. Remove from heat; add chopped tomatoes and cilantro. Toss with beans and adjust seasoning.

Preparation time: 25 minutes
Cooking time: 15 minutes
Yield: 4 servings

Nutrition information per serving:

Calories	80
Fat	4 g
Cholesterol	0 mg
Sodium	160 mg
Carbohydrate	11 g
Protein	3 g

White Beans with Escarole

Preparation time: 10 minutes

Cooking time: 10 to 12 minutes

Yield: 2 servings

Nutrition information per serving:

Calories	535
Fat	22 g
Cholesterol	0 mg
Sodium	540 mg
Carbohydrate	67 g
Protein	22 g

When each member of the Chicago Tribune *"Good Eating" staff was challenged to produce a quick but delicious dish using a supermarket convenience product, William Rice made this Italian dish from canned white beans and escarole.*

3 tablespoons olive oil, extra-virgin preferred
2 cloves garlic, peeled and coarsely chopped
⅛ teaspoon crushed red pepper flakes
1 small head escarole, torn into bite-sized pieces
1 19-ounce can white beans, Italian cannellini (white kidney) preferred, drained and rinsed
Salt to taste
Freshly ground pepper to taste
1½ to 2 teaspoons fresh lemon juice, or to taste

1. Heat oil, garlic, and red pepper flakes over medium-low heat in a high-sided pan or casserole until garlic turns golden, about 3 minutes. Add escarole and ¼ cup water; raise heat to medium-high. Stir to coat leaves with oil; cover. Cook until escarole has softened, stirring once, about 4 minutes.

2. Add beans; stir. Lower heat to medium; cover. Heat beans until warmed through, 4 to 5 minutes. Season with salt, pepper, and lemon juice. Portion into bowls or onto plates and serve.

Brown Cabbage

Ham is a Swedish smorgasbord basic (see Swedish Baked Ham, listed in Index), and brown cabbage (brunkal) goes with the ham. It's green cabbage that has been fried with a sweet brown syrup and then cooked in ham juices. The syrup is available at Swedish delis. Lyle's golden syrup can be used as well.

Preparation time: 10 minutes
Cooking time: 1 hour 20 minutes
Yield: 8 servings

4 to 5 tablespoons butter
1 large green cabbage, coarsely shredded
2 to 3 tablespoons Swedish light syrup (*ljus sirap*)
1½ to 2 cups pan juices from cooked ham or beef broth

1. Heat oven to 400°F. Melt butter in a large skillet. Brown cabbage in batches, about 10 minutes per batch, sprinkling with syrup during cooking.

2. Put browned cabbage in an ovenproof dish. Add ham juice to moisten. Bake, uncovered, stirring occasionally to prevent burning, until tender, about 1 hour. Cabbage can be made ahead, up to 3 days. Reheat before serving.

Nutrition information per serving (using beef broth):

Calories	105
Fat	7 g
Cholesterol	15 mg
Sodium	165 mg
Carbohydrate	11 g
Protein	2 g

Corn Curry

Preparation time: 30 minutes
Cooking time: 25 minutes
Yield: 4 servings

This vegetarian curry could be considered a "modern" Indian dish because chili peppers, corn, and tomatoes were introduced into this ancient cuisine only in the fifteenth and sixteenth centuries by the Portuguese. Yogita Pradhan of Des Plaines, Illinois, who cooks in the Maharashtrian (Bombay) tradition, provided the recipe.

Nutrition information per serving:

Calories	300
Fat	20 g
Cholesterol	0 mg
Sodium	465 mg
Carbohydrate	32 g
Protein	6 g

2 tablespoons vegetable oil
1 small onion, minced
1 to 3 fresh green chilies, minced
2 small dried red chilies, optional
1 teaspoon ground cumin
1 teaspoon ground coriander
¼ teaspoon ground black pepper
1 16-ounce package frozen corn
1 15-ounce can chopped tomatoes, undrained
½ teaspoon turmeric
½ teaspoon salt
¼ teaspoon ground red pepper or to taste
1 cup unsweetened coconut milk
Chopped cilantro

1. Heat oil in a large skillet or wok over medium heat. Add onion, green chilies, and dried chilies, if desired; sauté 3 minutes. Add cumin, coriander, and black pepper; cook, stirring, 3 minutes.

2. Stir in corn; cook, stirring often, 5 minutes. Add tomatoes with juice, turmeric, salt, and ground red pepper; cook 3 minutes.

3. Stir in coconut milk; cook until curry thickens slightly, about 10 minutes. Transfer to a serving dish; sprinkle with cilantro.

Pan-Seared Fennel and Carrots

This is healthful eating, Mediterranean style. Two flavorful vegetables cooked in a minimum of olive oil and accented with a dose of hot red pepper. The recipe was developed by food writer Pat Dailey of the Chicago Tribune.

1 tablespoon olive oil
⅛ to ¼ teaspoon crushed red pepper flakes, or to taste
1 onion, diced
1 fennel bulb, diced
½ pound peeled baby carrots, cut diagonally into thin
   slices
Salt to taste

1. Heat oil and red pepper flakes in a large skillet over high heat. When hot, add vegetables.

2. Cook, stirring occasionally, until tender and beginning to brown, about 8 minutes. Add salt to taste.

Preparation time: 20 minutes
Cooking time: 8 minutes
Yield: 4 servings

Nutrition information per serving:

Calories	85
Fat	4 g
Cholesterol	0 mg
Sodium	50 mg
Carbohydrate	12 g
Protein	2 g

Roasted Potatoes with Garlic and Rosemary

Preparation time: 15 minutes

Cooking time: 1 hour 15 minutes

Yield: 8 servings

Sally and Bill Sinacore of Palatine, Illinois, roasted two pork loins and a mammoth pan of these rosemary-and-garlic potatoes at their home for a 1996 gathering of a gourmet club to which they belong. This might be considered a fusion dish because, while the ethnic influence is Italian, the Yukon Gold potatoes were developed in Michigan.

Nutrition information per serving:

Calories	175
Fat	5 g
Cholesterol	0 mg
Sodium	6 mg
Carbohydrate	30 g
Protein	3 g

3 pounds Yukon Gold or red potatoes, cut in chunks
3 tablespoons olive oil
2 large cloves garlic, minced
2 tablespoons minced fresh rosemary
Salt to taste
Freshly ground pepper to taste

1. Heat oven to 325°F. Boil potatoes in a large saucepan of water until they begin to soften, 10 to 12 minutes. Drain well; transfer to a jelly-roll pan.

2. Mix oil, garlic, 1½ tablespoons rosemary, salt, and pepper. Drizzle over potatoes and toss lightly. Bake until potatoes are nicely browned, about 1 hour, stirring several times. Sprinkle remaining 1½ teaspoons rosemary and more salt and pepper over top.

Green Chili Potato Salad

American cuisine is a work in progress, always evolving to embrace the newest ethnic populations and to reflect current food trends. Here, Chicago Tribune columnist Pat Dailey fashions a fusion potato salad, using lemongrass and coconut milk from Thailand and spicy serrano chilies to make a salad ideally suited to summer.

Preparation time: 25 minutes

Cooking time: 12 to 15 minutes

Yield: 6 servings

2 pounds small red new potatoes
1 tablespoon vegetable oil
1 stalk lemongrass, trimmed and minced
1 to 2 serrano chilies, minced
¼ cup low-fat plain yogurt
2 tablespoons unsweetened coconut milk
Salt to taste
½ small sweet onion, finely diced
⅓ cup minced cilantro

Nutrition information per serving:

Calories	140
Fat	4 g
Cholesterol	1 mg
Sodium	13 mg
Carbohydrate	22 g
Protein	5 g

1. Put potatoes in a large saucepan with water to cover. Heat to a boil over high heat; cook until potatoes are just tender, 8 to 10 minutes. Drain well; set potatoes aside. Wipe out pan.

2. Heat oil in the same saucepan over medium-high heat. Add lemongrass and serranos. Cook, stirring until slightly softened, 1 minute. Remove from heat; transfer to a large bowl. Add yogurt, coconut milk, and salt.

3. Quarter potatoes; add to bowl along with onion and cilantro. Mix lightly. Serve at room temperature.

Potatoes and Anchovies

Preparation time: 40 minutes
Cooking time: 1 hour
Yield: 8 servings

Nutrition information per
serving:

Calories	250
Fat	18 g
Cholesterol	70 mg
Sodium	500 mg
Carbohydrate	17 g
Protein	7 g

As the sun goes down on Christmas Eve, the 300-year-old plank table in Kerstin and Joe Lane's dining room comes alive with candles set in bright red candleholders. This classic smorgasbord scalloped potato dish always appears on their table as well.

3 tablespoons butter
2 medium onions, julienned
4 medium Idaho potatoes, about 1½ pounds, peeled and
    cut into matchsticks
1 3½-ounce can Swedish anchovy fillets with brine
1¼ cups whipping cream

1. Heat oven to 400°F. Melt 1 tablespoon butter in a large skillet over medium heat. Add onions; cook until soft and lightly browned at edges, about 10 minutes.

2. Layer potatoes, onions, and anchovy fillets, finishing with a layer of potatoes, in a lightly buttered 9- or 10-inch gratin or baking dish. Pour 1 tablespoon of the brine from the anchovy can over mixture, if desired; dot top with remaining 2 tablespoons butter. Pour ¾ cup cream over the top.

3. Bake 45 minutes. Pour remaining ½ cup cream over the top; bake until potatoes are tender and browned, 10 to 15 minutes.

Peanut Potatoes

Freelance writer Colleen Taylor Sen explored the food of the agriculturally rich state of Maharashtra, located in central India (Bombay is the capital), through interviews with Maharashtrians living in the Chicago area. The cuisine is eclectic, featuring elements of the cooking of both north and south India, and rich with vegetable recipes such as this one.

1½ pounds small red potatoes
2 tablespoons vegetable oil
1 inch-long piece gingerroot, minced
1 teaspoon cumin seeds
¼ cup roasted unsalted peanuts, ground to a powder
1 tablespoon ground coriander
1 teaspoon ground cumin
½ teaspoon salt
¼ teaspoon ground red pepper
Grated coconut, chopped cilantro for garnish

1. Cook potatoes in boiling water to cover until tender, about 15 minutes. Drain. When cool enough to handle, peel; cut into 1½-inch cubes.

2. Heat oil in a large nonstick skillet over medium heat. Add ginger and cumin seeds; fry until seeds stop crackling, 2 to 3 minutes. Add potato cubes; cook, turning, until lightly browned, about 5 minutes.

3. Add ground peanuts, coriander, cumin, salt, and red pepper. Cook, tossing gently, 2 minutes; remove from heat. Garnish with coconut and cilantro.

Preparation time: 25 minutes
Cooking time: 30 minutes
Yield: 4 servings

Nutrition information per serving:

Calories	270
Fat	12 g
Cholesterol	0 mg
Sodium	280 mg
Carbohydrate	37 g
Protein	5 g

Turkish Stuffed Zucchini

Preparation time: 25 minutes
Cooking time: 30 minutes
Yield: 8 servings

Members of the International Cooking Club discovered this Turkish version of stuffed zucchini during a Middle Eastern dinner. This group is just one of many in the Chicago area that convene regularly and often try unfamiliar ethnic foods.

Nutrition information per serving:

Calories	140
Fat	11 g
Cholesterol	110 mg
Sodium	130 mg
Carbohydrate	4 g
Protein	7 g

4 medium zucchini, halved lengthwise
3 tablespoons unsalted butter
1 medium onion, finely chopped
3 small cloves garlic, minced
Salt to taste
Freshly ground pepper to taste
3 large eggs, lightly beaten
¾ cup (3 ounces) shredded Swiss cheese
½ cup (2 ounces) crumbled feta cheese
1½ tablespoons all-purpose flour
1 tablespoon chopped fresh dill
Paprika, about ¼ teaspoon

1. Heat oven to 375°F. Scoop out insides of zucchini with a spoon or melon baller, leaving a ½-inch rim. Place zucchini in a 9″ × 13″ baking dish; set aside. Chop scooped-out zucchini.

2. Melt butter in a skillet over medium-high heat. Add chopped zucchini, onion, and garlic. Cook, stirring often, until softened, 5 to 6 minutes. Add salt and pepper; transfer to a bowl. Lightly mix in eggs, cheeses, flour, and dill.

3. Spoon mixture into zucchini halves. Sprinkle with paprika. Bake until hot, 30 minutes. Serve hot or at room temperature.

Seared Zucchini with Three Peppers

Italian cooks have myriad ways to accent even the most familiar vegetables to make them taste fresh and exciting. Here, crushed red pepper and tangy bottled peperoncini peppers give pan-seared zucchini a spicy kiss. To tame the heat of the peperoncini, cut away and discard the seeds.

Preparation time: 15 minutes
Cooking time: 7 to 9 minutes
Yield: 4 servings

1 tablespoon olive oil
Pinch salt
Pinch crushed red pepper flakes
1 pound zucchini, sliced ¼ inch thick
2 peperoncini, minced and patted dry
1 teaspoon balsamic or red-wine vinegar
Freshly ground black pepper

Nutrition information per serving:

Calories	45
Fat	4 g
Cholesterol	0 mg
Sodium	35 mg
Carbohydrate	4 g
Protein	1 g

1. Heat oil, salt, and red pepper flakes in a large nonstick skillet over high heat until hot.

2. Add zucchini and peperoncini. Cook, stirring often, until zucchini begins to brown at edges, 6 to 7 minutes. Add vinegar and black pepper; cook 30 seconds. Add more salt to taste; serve.

Rice with Japanese Vegetables

Preparation time: 45 minutes
Standing time: 30 minutes
Cooking time: 25 minutes
Yield: 4 servings

Nutrition information per serving:

Calories	275
Fat	3 g
Cholesterol	45 mg
Sodium	430 mg
Carbohydrate	56 g
Protein	7 g

The diversity of flavors and the variety of vegetables in this dish are an example of why the Japanese have a low rate of heart disease and among the longest life spans in the world. Deep-fried tofu (aburage) is sold ready-made, and flaked seaweed is available in jars, both in Japanese markets.

Rice

1 cup Japanese-style rice
3¼ cups water
2 tablespoons soy sauce
2 teaspoons mirin (rice wine)
2 teaspoons sake
2 medium carrots, thinly sliced
4 slices lotus root
8 fresh shiitake mushrooms, stems removed and caps sliced
1 tablespoon rice vinegar, or more to taste
Salt to taste
1 large egg
1 teaspoon sugar
1 teaspoon vegetable oil

Garnish

½ cup diced deep-fried tofu, optional
Sliced pickled ginger
Seaweed flakes

1. Rinse rice in a strainer until water runs clear. Let drain 30 minutes. Place in a medium saucepan and add 1¼ cups water. Cover; heat to a simmer. Cook until tender, about 15 minutes.

2. Heat remaining 2 cups water to a boil in a large saucepan. Add soy sauce, mirin, and sake. Stir in carrots, lotus root, and mushrooms. Boil gently until most of the liquid has evaporated and carrots are fork-tender, about 10 minutes.

3. Transfer rice to a large bowl. Add vinegar and salt; toss gently to mix. Add vegetables to rice; add enough of their cooking liquid to flavor and moisten rice. Toss gently.

4. Beat egg and sugar in a small dish. Heat oil in a small skillet; add egg mixture, swirling pan to spread egg. Cook until set, 30 to 40 seconds. Transfer to a plate to cool. Roll up; slice into thin strips. Sprinkle over rice.

5. Garnish with fried tofu, ginger, and a sprinkling of seaweed flakes. Serve at room temperature.

Rice with Pigeon Peas

Preparation time: 10 minutes
Cooking time: 20 minutes
Yield: 6 servings

Nutrition information per serving:

Calories	510
Fat	11 g
Cholesterol	0 mg
Sodium	920 mg
Carbohydrate	90 g
Protein	11 g

Arroz con gandules is a traditional Puerto Rican rice dish. This one is adapted from a recipe by Lucy Garcia, Christian Cruz, and José Garcia of Chicago, who shared it with the Chicago Tribune Magazine *during the 1993 holiday season. Sazon is a seasoning mix available in the imported-foods section of large supermarkets and at most Hispanic markets. This dish often accompanies tamales, fried plantains, or morcillas (blood sausage).*

¼ cup vegetable oil
1 small onion, chopped
1 0.17-ounce envelope sazon or 2 teaspoons Creole
   seasoning
1 small tomato, chopped
1 tablespoon chopped green olives
1 tablespoon chopped pimiento
1 teaspoon chopped capers
1 teaspoon salt
3 cups long-grain rice
1 15- to 16-ounce can pigeon peas, rinsed and drained
½ cup tomato sauce
4½ cups water

1. Heat oil in a 3-quart saucepan over medium heat. Add onion; cook 2 minutes. Add sazon, tomato, olives, pimiento, capers, and salt. Stir well.

2. Add rice. Stir to coat with oil; cook 1 minute. Add pigeon peas and tomato sauce; mix well. Stir in water. Heat to a boil; cover. Reduce heat to simmer. Cook until rice is tender, about 15 minutes. Fluff with a fork.

Mexican Red Rice

Chicago internist John La Puma, M.D., believes that good-for-you food needs to taste good first. Director of the Cooking, Healthy Eating and Fitness (CHEF) program at Alexian Brothers Medical Center in Elk Grove Village, Illinois, La Puma often works the line at Topolobampo. La Puma says that chef Rick Bayless "values flavor as much as anything." One of La Puma's creations is this healthful recipe for Mexican rice. It's low in fat and cholesterol, but provides plenty of sizzle.

1 cup brown rice

2 cups prepared good-quality tomato salsa

2 teaspoons salt

2 teaspoons crushed Mexican oregano

3 onions, cut into 1-inch pieces

3 large green bell peppers, seeded and cut into 1-inch pieces

12 cloves garlic, halved

1 13¾-ounce can vegetable or chicken broth

Salt to taste

Ground black pepper to taste

4 green onions, chopped

¼ cup minced cilantro

1. Cook rice over medium-high heat in a large, heavy skillet until deeply aromatic, lightly browned, and popping regularly, about 5 minutes. Add salsa, salt, and oregano; simmer 1 minute. Top with onions, peppers, and garlic. Add broth; stir well.

2. Reduce heat; cover. Simmer 45 minutes. Remove from heat. If still slightly soupy, cover and let sit a few minutes until liquid is absorbed. Season with salt and pepper. Fluff with a fork; stir in green onions and cilantro.

Preparation time: 30 minutes

Cooking time: 50 minutes

Yield: 8 servings

Nutrition information per serving:

Calories	215
Fat	4 g
Cholesterol	1 mg
Sodium	1,380 mg
Carbohydrate	40 g
Protein	6 g

VARIATIONS

Add a chipotle, morita, or other dried whole chili with the liquid; or add 4 cups shredded cabbage, kale, Swiss chard, or beet greens during the last 10 minutes of cooking.

Indian-Spiced Rice Pilaf

Preparation time: 5 minutes

Cooking time: 20 minutes

Yield: 4 servings

Scan the recipes in an Indian cookbook, and two things become clear: Dishes with twenty or more ingredients are pretty common, and so are intricate preparations and lengthy cooking times. These traits conspire to keep Indian cooking off-limits for many cooks. But this Indian-flavored pilaf needs only a handful of spices. Serve it with sautéed chicken breast or shrimp.

Nutrition information per serving:

Calories	195
Fat	0.5 g
Cholesterol	0 mg
Sodium	530 mg
Carbohydrate	41 g
Protein	5 g

1 cup basmati or Texmati rice

2 cups reduced-sodium chicken broth or water

½ teaspoon ground cumin

¼ teaspoon ground cardamom (optional)

¼ teaspoon ground red pepper

1 bay leaf

½ teaspoon salt

1 tablespoon minced fresh mint

1. Combine all ingredients except mint in a medium saucepan. Heat to a boil over medium-high heat. Cover and reduce heat; simmer until liquid is absorbed, 17 to 20 minutes. Remove bay leaf. Stir in mint.

Toasted Orzo and Rice Pilaf

Greeks love grains and use them liberally as beds for grilled meats, poultry, and fish. Although the orzo and rice are sautéed together in this recipe from Chicago Tribune columnist Abby Mandel, only the orzo browns. The browning, together with the nutty flavor of basmati rice, makes this a rich-tasting dish. The pilaf can be made a day ahead and reheated in the oven. Add the lemon juice and dill just before serving.

1 tablespoon olive oil
¾ cup orzo
¾ cup basmati rice
1 small shallot, minced
3½ cups reduced-sodium chicken broth, fat skimmed
Scant ½ teaspoon salt
Freshly ground pepper
1 teaspoon fresh lemon juice
¾ cup loosely packed chopped fresh dill

1. Heat oil in a heavy 4-quart saucepan over medium-high heat. Add orzo and rice. Cook, stirring often, until orzo is browned, about 5 minutes. Add shallot; cook 1 minute, stirring often. Add broth, salt, and pepper. Simmer, covered, over low heat until all liquid is absorbed, about 15 minutes. Let rest off heat, covered, 10 minutes. Stir in lemon juice and dill. Adjust seasoning.

Preparation time: 20 minutes
Cooking time: 30 minutes
Yield: 6 servings

Nutrition information per serving:

Calories	186
Fat	3 g
Cholesterol	0 mg
Sodium	505 mg
Carbohydrate	34 g
Protein	6 g

Chive Couscous

Preparation time: 10 minutes

Cooking time: 3 minutes

Standing time: 10 minutes

Yield: 4 servings

Nutrition information per serving:

Calories	135
Fat	4 g
Cholesterol	0 mg
Sodium	115 mg
Carbohydrate	22 g
Protein	4 g

This recipe uses Moroccan couscous, one of the great time-savers. It is no more difficult to prepare than boiling water. The couscous is mixed with bright green chives for color and an oil-and-vinegar dressing for flavor.

½ cup tomato vegetable juice (such as V-8)
½ cup water
1 cup quick-cooking couscous
¼ cup snipped fresh chives
1 tablespoon seasoned rice vinegar
1 tablespoon extra-virgin olive oil
Salt to taste
Ground red pepper to taste

1. Heat vegetable juice and water to a boil in a small saucepan or 4-cup microwave-safe dish. Remove from heat; stir in couscous. Cover; let stand 10 minutes.

2. Fluff with a fork to separate grains; add remaining ingredients and mix well.

Avocado Tomato Relish

Memories of dining in Mexico often include savoring the piquant sauces, dips, and relishes that accompany many grilled items in that country's restaurants. This recipe for a highly versatile relish (try it with chicken, pork, fish, or even eggs) features the avocado. To peel an avocado with minimum loss of the flesh beneath the skin, cut round it lengthwise and twist to separate it into halves. Insert the point of your knife into the pit and twist gently to remove it. Cut each piece of avocado in half lengthwise, then carefully peel back the skin and discard.

2 small, ripe avocados, peeled, pitted, and diced
1 cup quartered cherry or cocktail tomatoes
4 green onions, thinly sliced
1 jalapeño pepper, seeded and minced
3 tablespoons minced cilantro
1 tablespoon fresh lime juice
Salt to taste

1. Combine all ingredients in a bowl and mix lightly.

Preparation time: 15 minutes
Yield: 6 servings

Nutrition information per serving:

Calories	125
Fat	10 g
Cholesterol	0 mg
Sodium	13 mg
Carbohydrate	8 g
Protein	2 g

Cilantro Chutney

Preparation time: 15 minutes

Yield: 1 cup

For those who have experienced the exotic smells and looked over the mysterious ingredients on display at the Indian markets that line Chicago's Devon Avenue, it is exciting to learn how they are used in the kitchen. Here is a delightfully tangy Indian condiment.

Nutrition information per 2 tablespoons:

Calories	8
Fat	0 g
Cholesterol	0 mg
Sodium	2 mg
Carbohydrate	2 g
Protein	0.5 g

1½ cups cilantro leaves
2 tablespoons fresh mint leaves
⅓ cup water
3 jalapeño chilies, seeded
1 inch-long piece gingerroot, peeled
1 tablespoon fresh lime juice or more to taste
Salt to taste

1. Combine all ingredients in a blender; puree. Can be refrigerated up to 2 days.

Breads

Ann's Bakery, Milwaukee Avenue

Quick Smoky Corn Muffins

Preparation time: 5 minutes

Cooking time: 20 minutes

Yield: 6 muffins

Nutrition information per muffin:

Calories	165
Fat	7 g
Cholesterol	65 mg
Sodium	370 mg
Carbohydrate	21 g
Protein	6 g

These muffins accompanied a Colombian chicken and potato stew (see Index) in the Chicago Tribune's "Fast Food" *column in February 1996. The sauce from canned chipotle chilies, which are smoked jalapeño peppers, gives them a whiff of the grill.*

1 8½-ounce box corn muffin mix

1 large egg

⅓ cup milk

1 to 2 teaspoons sauce from canned chipotle chilies in adobo sauce

¼ cup shredded Monterey Jack or cheddar cheese

1. Heat oven to 400°F. Combine all ingredients in a medium bowl; mix lightly.

2. Divide batter among 6 greased or paper muffin cups, filling half full. Bake until puffy and set, 18 to 20 minutes. Serve warm.

Australian Scones

Reader Robert Cornish sent the Chicago Tribune *this recipe for breakfast scones, noting that it's the easiest biscuit recipe he's ever found. Although scones can be made plain, we like these best with currants and a little sugar added to the dough. Whichever way you decide, be sure to eat them warm, spread with a little butter, honey, lemon curd, or fruit preserves.*

4½ cups all-purpose flour
2 tablespoons sugar
4 teaspoons baking powder
¼ teaspoon salt
2 cups half-and-half
1 cup dried currants or raisins

1. Heat oven to 400°F. Combine flour, sugar, baking powder, and salt in a large mixing bowl. Make a well in the center. Add half-and-half. Stir until batter forms. Mix in currants.

2. Transfer dough to a floured board. Shape into a ¾-inch-thick circle. Cut out rounds with a 2-inch biscuit cutter. Transfer to two greased baking sheets. Bake until lightly colored, about 20 minutes. Serve warm.

Preparation time: 20 minutes
Cooking time: 20 minutes
Yield: 20 scones

Nutrition information per serving:

Calories	160
Fat	3 g
Cholesterol	9 mg
Sodium	135 mg
Carbohydrate	30 g
Protein	4 g

New Year's Pretzels

Preparation time: 25 minutes

Rising time: 3 hours 45 minutes

Cooking time: 20 minutes

Yield: 12 pretzels

Nutrition information per pretzel:

Calories	330
Fat	8 g
Cholesterol	3 mg
Sodium	400 mg
Carbohydrate	59 g
Protein	6 g

NOTE

Look for rose water in specialty food stores and Middle Eastern markets. Lemon juice can be used instead.

Iowa's Amana Colonies, founded by a German religious sect in 1855, fed members in austere communal dining halls, overseen by "kitchen bosses," until the 1930s. Everyone looked forward to holidays and a break in the monotony of the set weekly menu. Easter would bring dumpling soup, Thanksgiving a fruit kuchen, and Christmas meant stollen and lebkuchen, or honey cake. New Year's was marked by the baking of these iced pretzels called neujahrsbrezel. This dough will keep in the refrigerator for five days; portions can be cut off as needed.

Pretzels

1 cup whole milk

½ cup sugar

1 small (0.6-ounce) cake fresh yeast or 1 package active dry yeast

1 cup warm water (105 to 115°F)

5 to 6 cups all-purpose flour

2 teaspoons salt

6 tablespoons vegetable shortening, melted

Rose Water Icing

1 cup confectioners' sugar

4 teaspoons milk or warm water

½ teaspoon rose water, see Note

1. Scald milk with sugar in a medium saucepan. Cool to lukewarm; transfer to a large bowl. Dissolve yeast in warm water; add to cooled milk. Add 3 cups flour and salt; beat until smooth. Add melted shortening and enough of the remaining flour to make a soft, smooth dough. Knead until supple and elastic, 8 to 10 minutes. Place in a greased bowl; turn to coat. Cover; set in a warm place away from drafts. Let rise until double in bulk, about 3 hours.

2. Divide dough into 12 equal portions. Roll each portion into a rope about ¼ inch thick and 12 inches long; twist into the form of a pretzel. Place on a greased baking sheet. Cover loosely; let rise again until light, 35 to 45 minutes. Heat oven to 425°F. Bake until golden, about 20 minutes. Transfer to a cooling rack.

3. Stir icing ingredients together in a small bowl to form a thick paste. Ice pretzels while still warm.

Hot Cross Buns

Preparation time: 45 minutes

Rising time: 2½ hours

Cooking time: 25 minutes

Yield: 24 rolls

Mary Meade, a pen name used by the late Chicago Tribune *food editor Ruth Ellen Church, guided many Chicago-area cooks from the 1940s through the 1960s. A reader in 1992, recalling Mary Meade's expertise, wrote just before Easter to request a rerun of her recipe for hot cross buns. These small yeast rolls with a cross of white icing traditionally are served in Britain and in the United States on Good Friday.*

Nutrition information per bun:

Calories	135
Fat	2 g
Cholesterol	6 mg
Sodium	120 mg
Carbohydrate	26 g
Protein	3 g

Rolls

1 package active dry yeast or one small (0.6-ounce) cake fresh yeast

⅓ cup sugar

¼ cup warm water (105 to 115°F)

3½ to 4 cups all-purpose flour

1 teaspoon salt

1 teaspoon cinnamon

¼ teaspoon ground allspice

1 large egg

1 cup whole milk

½ cup raisins or dried currants

¼ cup butter or solid vegetable shortening, melted

Icing

1½ cups confectioners' sugar

1 teaspoon pure vanilla extract or lemon juice

2 to 3 tablespoons milk

1. For rolls, stir yeast and 1 teaspoon sugar into the warm water in a small bowl; let mixture stand until foamy, 5 to 10 minutes.

2. Combine 3½ cups flour, remaining sugar, salt, cinnamon, and allspice in a large bowl. Lightly beat egg and milk in another small bowl. Add liquid ingredients to dry ingredients; stir to make dough. Add raisins. Slowly mix in melted butter. The dough should be soft and a little sticky but not wet. Add additional flour if dough is too sticky.

3. Turn dough out onto a floured surface; knead until dough is smooth, supple, and elastic, about 10 minutes. Transfer to a large oiled bowl; turn to coat all sides. Cover with a damp towel; let rise in a warm spot until dough has doubled, 1½ to 2 hours.

4. Punch dough down; divide into 24 equal pieces. Shape each piece into a smooth ball. Cut an X in the top of each bun using kitchen shears. Place in a greased jelly-roll pan with sides lightly touching. Cover with a damp cloth; let rise until doubled, 35 to 45 minutes.

5. Heat oven to 400°F. Bake buns until golden, 22 to 25 minutes. Transfer to a cooling rack.

6. For frosting, sift confectioners' sugar into a small bowl. Add vanilla and enough milk to make a thin icing. Drizzle icing into each X.

Easter Babka

Preparation time: 30 minutes

Rising time: 4 hours

Cooking time: 50 minutes

Yield: 4 loaves, 16 slices each

Nutrition information per
slice:

Calories	115
Fat	4 g
Cholesterol	50 mg
Sodium	45 mg
Carbohydrate	16 g
Protein	3 g

Darka Iwachiw shared her recipe for babka, a yeast bread that is a Ukrainian tradition. The bread goes into her large Easter basket with sausages, ham, pots of farmer cheese, and butter. The whole is blessed with other members' baskets in Sts. Volodymyr and Olha Ukrainian Catholic Parish in Chicago. Iwachiw grew up watching her Ukrainian-born mother bake the bread, which can be elaborately designed with braids, rosettes, crosses, and little doves. Iwachiw now speeds the preparation by using a food processor to knead the dough.

1 large (2-ounce) cake fresh yeast or 4 packages active
   dry yeast
1 cup plus 1 teaspoon sugar
½ cup warm water (105 to 115°F)
6 whole eggs
8 egg yolks
Grated zest of 1 orange
1 teaspoon pure vanilla extract
1 teaspoon salt
2 cups milk at room temperature
8 to 9½ cups all-purpose flour
1 cup (2 sticks) unsalted butter, melted
1 cup golden raisins, optional
Finely crushed bread crumbs

1. Crumble yeast into a small bowl; add 1 teaspoon sugar and the warm water. Let stand until foamy, 5 minutes.

2. Mix 5 eggs and the egg yolks, remaining 1 cup sugar, orange zest, vanilla, and salt in a large bowl. Add milk and yeast mixture; mix well. Add 8 cups flour; mix to form dough; add more flour as necessary to make a soft but not wet dough. Knead on a floured surface until dough is supple and elastic, 10 to 15 minutes. Slowly add melted butter. Continue kneading until butter is completely absorbed. Knead in raisins, if using.

3. Place dough in a greased bowl. Cover the bowl with a damp towel; let rise in a warm spot until doubled, 1 to 1½ hours. Punch dough down; cover and let rise again until more than doubled, 1 to 1½ hours.

4. Grease the insides of four 2-pound 7-ounce coffee cans. Line the bottom of each with a circle of wax paper; line the sides with waxed paper, extending it 2 inches beyond the top of each can. Grease the paper; sprinkle with bread crumbs. Divide dough into four portions to fill each can about ⅓ full. Cover loosely with a damp cloth; let rise until dough almost fills the cans, about 1 hour.

5. Heat oven to 325°F. Beat remaining egg; brush tops of loaves with egg. Bake until golden, 45 to 50 minutes. Turn off oven; let loaves rest in oven 15 minutes with door ajar. Gently remove loaves from cans; let cool on a thick terry towel, moving them as little as possible while still warm.

Braided Easter Bread

Preparation time: 30 minutes

Rising time: 2¼ hours

Cooking time: 35 minutes

Yield: 1 large loaf, 20 slices

Nutrition information per slice:

Calories	180
Fat	6 g
Cholesterol	55 mg
Sodium	70 mg
Carbohydrate	26 g
Protein	5 g

Chicago Tribune food and wine columnist William Rice visited the suburban Athens home of his friend Nikos Georgulas in time for Greek Easter in 1995. The daylong Easter Sunday feast included spit-roasted goat, feta and kaseri cheeses, olives, and artichokes in dill. But the morning began with a basket of scarlet eggs and this special Easter bread, eaten with Attica honey.

¾ cup milk

½ cup (1 stick) unsalted butter, softened

½ cup sugar

½ teaspoon salt

¼ teaspoon finely crushed anise seeds

¼ teaspoon ground cinnamon

1 package (2½ teaspoons) active dry yeast

3 tablespoons warm water (105 to 115°F)

1 teaspoon honey

4 large eggs

About 4¼ cups all-purpose flour

1 tablespoon sesame seeds

1. Heat milk in a saucepan until hot but not simmering. Remove from heat; stir in butter, sugar, salt, anise seeds, and cinnamon. Cool to lukewarm.

2. Meanwhile, combine yeast with 3 tablespoons lukewarm water and honey in a large mixing bowl or the large bowl of an electric mixer fitted with a dough hook. Let stand until bubbly, about 5 minutes.

3. Stir lukewarm milk mixture into yeast mixture. Beat 3 eggs lightly; add to the liquids. Begin beating in flour, ½ cup at a time, until 4 cups have been added. Turn dough out onto a lightly floured work surface to knead in remaining ¼ cup flour. Gently knead soft dough until smooth and elastic, about 5 minutes.

4. Transfer dough to a large greased bowl. Cover with plastic wrap; set aside at room temperature until doubled in bulk, about 1½ hours.

5. Return dough to the work surface. Divide into 3 equal pieces. Roll each piece into a "rope" about 20 inches long. Pinch 3 end pieces together and braid the strands of dough tightly. Curl the braid into a ring, pinching and tucking loose ends together.

6. Transfer the ring to a greased or parchment paper–lined baking sheet. Cover the braid loosely with plastic wrap; let rise at room temperature until doubled in bulk, about 45 minutes.

7. Heat oven to 350°F. Beat the remaining egg with 1 tablespoon water in a small bowl. Brush dough evenly with egg wash. Sprinkle with sesame seeds. Bake in the middle of the oven until the crust is golden brown, about 35 minutes. Cool bread on a wire rack.

Irish Soda Bread

Preparation time: 20 minutes

Cooking time: 50 to 60
    minutes

Yield: 1 large loaf, 26 slices

Nutrition information per
slice:

Calories	145
Fat	3 g
Cholesterol	15 mg
Sodium	105 mg
Carbohydrate	28 g
Protein	3 g

*For those who are Irish born or of Irish descent—and more than
1 million people in the Chicago area are, according to census
figures—soda bread is a celebratory staple. In 1992, Margaret
Sullivan of Chicago shared her recipe with the* Chicago
Tribune *just before St. Patrick's Day. This bread is best served
the day it is made.*

4 cups all-purpose flour
1 cup sugar
1 teaspoon baking soda
1 teaspoon baking powder
¼ teaspoon salt
1⅓ cups buttermilk
⅓ cup unsalted butter, melted
1 large egg, lightly beaten
1 cup raisins or dried currants

1. Heat oven to 350°F. Combine flour, sugar, baking soda,
   baking powder, and salt in a large bowl; make a well in the
   center. Combine buttermilk, butter, and egg in a smaller
   bowl. Pour the liquid into the well of dry ingredients; stir
   to form a soft dough. Add raisins; mix lightly.

2. Transfer batter to a greased 9- to 10-inch cast-iron skillet
   or large baking sheet. Shape into a ball. Cut an X across
   the top. Bake until set, 50 to 60 minutes.

Desserts

Making pierogi, Ukranian Village

Ginger Plum Cake

Preparation time: 15 minutes
Cooking time: 30 minutes
Yield: 6 servings

Nutrition information per serving:

Calories	270
Fat	13 g
Cholesterol	155 mg
Sodium	255 mg
Carbohydrate	36 g
Protein	3 g

Here's an ideal finale to a traditional German meal, a lovely autumnal cake that can be made quickly from tart red plums, spices, and a boxed mix. The fresh fruit and ginger will reawaken dormant appetites. Pat Dailey, who included this recipe in a "Fast Food" column in the Chicago Tribune, *points out that this creation can masquerade quite nicely as a homemade cake.*

2 tablespoons unsalted butter
2 to 3 plums, pitted and sliced
2 tablespoons sugar
1 small box (7½ ounces, such as Jiffy) yellow cake mix
1 large egg
½ cup sour cream
1 teaspoon pure vanilla extract
1 teaspoon ground ginger

1. Heat oven to 325°F. Melt butter in oven in an 8-inch round metal cake pan. Arrange plum slices over bottom of pan in a circular design. Sprinkle with sugar. Cook over medium heat until plums begin to give off some juice, 3 to 4 minutes. Remove from heat.

2. Combine cake mix, egg, sour cream, vanilla, and ginger in a large bowl. Stir until smooth. Pour over plums.

3. Bake until a wooden pick inserted in the center comes out clean, about 25 minutes. Loosen cake from sides of pan and invert onto a serving plate. Serve warm.

Cardamom Cream Cake

Pound cakes flavored with cardamom are popular in Scandinavia. It's best to grind your own cardamom, because the kind that is sold ground quickly loses its flavor. This cake is adapted from a recipe in Scandinavian Feasts by Beatrice Ojakangas.

Preparation time: 20 minutes
Cooking time: 60 minutes
Yield: 10 servings

2 cups all-purpose flour
1 cup sugar
2 teaspoons baking powder
1 teaspoon freshly ground cardamom, see note
⅛ teaspoon salt
3 large eggs, at room temperature
1½ cups whipping cream
Confectioners' sugar

Nutrition information per serving:

Calories	315
Fat	15 g
Cholesterol	105 mg
Sodium	155 mg
Carbohydrate	41 g
Protein	5 g

1. Heat oven to 350°F. Combine flour, sugar, baking powder, cardamom, and salt in the large bowl of an electric mixer. Blend in eggs at low speed. Add cream; beat at high speed, scraping bowl, until batter is texture of softly whipped cream.

2. Turn batter into a 9-inch buttered and floured tube pan. Bake until a wooden skewer inserted into the center of the cake comes out clean, 50 to 60 minutes. Cool 5 minutes in pan. Invert onto wire rack; cool completely. Dust with confectioners' sugar before serving.

NOTE

Cardamom pods are sold in jars in the spice section of large supermarkets or in Swedish or Indian markets. The pods can be finely ground in an electric spice grinder or coffee grinder.

Lemon Yogurt Cake

Preparation time: 30 minutes
Cooking time: 1 hour
Yield: 10 servings

Nutrition information per serving:

Calories	640
Fat	22 g
Cholesterol	120 mg
Sodium	430 mg
Carbohydrate	101 g
Protein	8 g

"I think Greek is going to become a very popular cuisine; it's such a cozy food," cookbook author Paula Wolfert told the Chicago Tribune *in 1992. "People talk about home cooking, and Greek food is home cooking; it's soothing, comforting food."* And so it is, especially this cake from Papagus Greek Taverna.

Cake
3 cups all-purpose flour
1 tablespoon baking powder
1 teaspoon baking soda
½ teaspoon salt
1 cup (2 sticks) unsalted butter, softened
2 cups sugar
3 large eggs, separated
1¾ cups plain yogurt
Grated zest of 2 lemons
1 teaspoon pure vanilla extract

Syrup
1½ cups sugar
1½ cups water
⅓ cup Metaxa or brandy

1. Heat oven to 350°F. Sift together flour, baking powder, baking soda, and salt; set aside.

2. Cream butter and sugar in the large bowl of an electric mixer on high speed. Add egg yolks, one at a time, mixing well after each addition. Stop the mixer; add yogurt, lemon zest, and vanilla. Mix just to combine. Fold in sifted dry ingredients.

3. Beat egg whites in a clean bowl until they hold soft peaks; gently fold into batter. Transfer to a buttered, floured 10-inch bundt pan. Bake until a toothpick inserted in the center comes out clean, about 1 hour.

4. For syrup, combine sugar and water in a saucepan. Heat to a boil; reduce heat. Simmer 20 minutes. Remove from heat; add Metaxa.

5. Cool cake in the pan on a wire rack 15 minutes. Brush with syrup, adding it only as fast as it is absorbed. Cool cake completely in the pan. Invert onto a plate. Cut in slices to serve.

Spiced Honey Cake

Preparation time: 30 minutes
Cooking time: 1 hour
Yield: 12 servings

Nutrition information per serving:

Calories	340
Fat	13 g
Cholesterol	75 mg
Sodium	215 mg
Carbohydrate	54 g
Protein	6 g

Chicago's Ukrainian Village is one of the city's strongest ethnic communities. Chicago Tribune *reporter Steven Pratt toured the area and discovered that shops selling food to take home were a big business in the village. He found the greatest variety of baked goods at Ann's Bakery, where the first thing you see is shelves of unfamiliar breads. Also tempting are the multilayer cakes; the strawberry, cream, and apple pastries; and spiced cakes such as this one. This dense cake, called* medivnyk, *is fragrant with warm spices and studded with dried fruits. Make it one or two days ahead so the flavors can develop.*

¾ cup honey
2 3-inch strips lemon zest
2 3-inch strips orange zest
1 teaspoon baking soda
1 teaspoon cinnamon
¼ teaspoon allspice
¼ teaspoon salt
½ cup (1 stick) unsalted butter, softened
½ cup packed light-brown sugar
3 large eggs
2 tablespoons sour cream
1 teaspoon pure vanilla extract
2 cups all-purpose flour
1 teaspoon baking powder
1¼ cups dried fruit, preferably equal parts raisins, currants, and dried cherries
½ cup chopped walnuts

1. Heat oven to 325°F. Combine honey and citrus zest in a small saucepan; heat to a boil. Remove from heat; add baking soda, cinnamon, allspice, and salt. Set aside to cool. Remove zest; discard.

2. Beat butter and sugar in the large bowl of an electric mixer on high speed until light, 2 minutes. Add eggs, one at a time, mixing well after each addition. Add honey mixture, sour cream, and vanilla; mix well. Add flour and baking powder; mix lightly. Add dried fruit and nuts. Mix just until combined.

3. Transfer to a greased 9″ × 5″ × 3″ loaf pan. Bake until a toothpick inserted in the center comes out clean, about 1 hour. Cool in the pan 5 minutes; invert onto a wire rack. Cool.

Peach Kuchen

Preparation time: 45 minutes

Cooking time: About 1 hour

Yield: 8 servings

Nutrition information per serving:

Calories	360
Fat	18 g
Cholesterol	95 mg
Sodium	75 mg
Carbohydrate	48 g
Protein	4 g

The Chicago Tribune Test Kitchen Director Alicia Tessling answered a reader's request by finding this German coffee cake, kuchen, in the Chicago Tribune's archives. Originally from an Abby Mandel column, it's the perfect summertime dessert. To ripen peaches, place them in a paper bag on a counter for a day or two; once they have ripened, store them in the refrigerator. Other fruit, such as plums or cherries, can be substituted.

Crust

1¼ cups all-purpose flour

¼ cup sugar

¼ teaspoon ground ginger

¼ teaspoon salt

⅛ teaspoon cinnamon

½ cup plus 2 tablespoons (1¼ sticks) cold, unsalted butter, cut into small pieces

Filling

6 to 8 medium ripe peaches

⅔ cup sugar

⅓ cup sour cream

2 large egg yolks

3 tablespoons all-purpose flour

1½ teaspoons pure vanilla extract

Whipped cream, optional

1. Heat oven to 400°F. For the crust, put flour, sugar, ginger, salt, and cinnamon into a food processor fitted with a metal blade. Process to mix. Sprinkle butter over flour. Process until mixture resembles coarse crumbs. (Or mix dry ingredients in a large bowl; cut in butter with a pastry blender or two knives until mixture resembles coarse crumbs.)

2. Refrigerate ½ cup crumb mixture for topping. Pat remaining crumb mixture evenly over the bottom and sides of a greased 10-inch round tart pan with a removable bottom. Put the pan onto a baking sheet. Bake until golden, 18 to 20 minutes. Remove from oven; cool on a wire rack.

3. Reduce oven temperature to 350°F. For the filling, drop peaches into a large pot of boiling water just until their skins slip off easily, 30 to 60 seconds. Cool by running under cold water. Remove skin. Cut peaches in half; remove pits. Cut each half into ¼-inch-thick slices. Arrange slices attractively over the cooled crust.

4. Mix sugar, sour cream, egg yolks, flour, and vanilla in a medium bowl. Carefully pour over peaches. Sprinkle with reserved crumb mixture. Bake until filling is set and crumbs are slightly golden, 40 to 50 minutes. Cool on a wire rack. Serve warm with whipped cream, if desired.

Irish Whiskey Pie

Preparation time: 1 hour

Cooking time: 30 minutes

Chilling time: 4½ hours

Yield: One 9-inch pie

   (8 servings)

Nutrition information per serving:

Calories	415
Fat	25 g
Cholesterol	180 mg
Sodium	216 mg
Carbohydrate	38 g
Protein	7 g

Irish whiskey pie is a familiar favorite on St. Patrick's Day menus. The Irish make whiskey of rare quality, and a few ounces of it transform an unexceptional cream pie into something ethereal. Indeed, the better the whiskey, the better the taste. "But do not use Scotch!" a leprechaun told Chicago Tribune *columnist William Rice. "If you do, surely the filling will curdle."*

Pastry

1½ cups all-purpose flour

½ teaspoon salt

½ cup (1 stick) cold unsalted butter

4 to 5 tablespoons cold water

Filling

¾ cup sugar

1 envelope unflavored gelatin

1 cup whipping cream

⅓ cup Irish whiskey

4 large eggs, separated

Salt

1 teaspoon pure vanilla extract

⅛ teaspoon nutmeg

1. Heat oven to 375°F. Combine flour and salt in a medium bowl; cut in butter until mixture resembles coarse crumbs. Add water, a tablespoon at a time, until dough clings together. Shape into a flat disk, cover with plastic wrap; refrigerate at least 30 minutes.

2. Roll dough on a lightly floured surface into a 10-inch circle; fit into a 9-inch pie plate. Cover dough with a sheet of aluminum foil and fill with dried beans or pie weights. Bake 20 minutes. Remove beans and foil; continue to bake until light golden, about 10 minutes. Set aside to cool.

3. For the filling, combine ½ cup sugar and the gelatin in the top of a double boiler. Stir in ⅔ cup whipping cream and the Irish whiskey. Stir over boiling water until mixture begins to simmer. Remove top pan; set aside.

4. Beat egg yolks with a pinch of salt in a medium bowl. Stirring constantly, slowly pour about half the cream mixture into yolks. Pour back into remaining cream mixture. Place top pan back over boiling water; stir over medium heat until liquid thickens. Continue to cook 1 minute. Transfer top pan to a bowl filled with ice cubes and water. Stir in vanilla and nutmeg. Allow mixture to cool, stirring occasionally, until it begins to set.

5. Whip remaining ⅓ cup cream with a pinch of salt until soft peaks form. Whip egg whites with a pinch of salt in a clean bowl until frothy. Slowly add remaining ¼ cup sugar, beating until soft peaks form. Fold whipped cream into chilled custard; fold in egg whites. Pour into prepared pastry shell; chill 4 to 6 hours.

Maple Syrup Pie

Preparation time: 30 minutes

Baking time: 30 minutes

Yield: One 8-inch pie

    (6 servings)

Nutrition information per serving:

Calories	350
Fat	16 g
Cholesterol	10 mg
Sodium	165 mg
Carbohydrate	50 g
Protein	4 g

In the Canadian province of Quebec, local maple syrup is used by cooks to give a sweet, velvety quality to food. The following recipe comes from the farmhouse restaurant Sucrerie de la Montagne. Store maple products in the refrigerator or the freezer. If put in the freezer, they won't freeze, just thicken, but will keep for years.

2 tablespoons butter

¼ cup all-purpose flour

1 cup pure maple syrup

½ cup water

½ cup chopped walnuts

1 8-inch unbaked pie shell

Whipped cream, optional

1. Heat oven to 425°F. Melt butter in a medium saucepan over medium heat. Stir in flour. Cook, stirring, until flour browns slightly. Stir in maple syrup and water. Cook, stirring, until mixture thickens. Remove from heat; let cool. Stir in nuts.

2. Pour mixture into pie shell. Bake 10 minutes. Reduce oven temperature to 350°F. Bake until crust is golden and filling is brown, about 20 minutes. Cool on a wire rack. Serve at room temperature with a dollop of whipped cream if desired.

Fruit Strudel

Janos Kiss, former executive chef at the Hyatt Regency Chicago, shared this strudel from his native Hungary with Chicago Tribune readers. He used apples for the filling, but any type of fruit in season can be substituted.

5 sheets phyllo dough
¼ cup (½ stick) unsalted butter, melted
½ cup coarse bread crumbs
2 pounds fruit of your choice, such as apples or pears, peeled and sliced
¼ cup sugar
⅓ cup ground walnuts
Pinch cinnamon
Melted butter

Preparation time: 35 minutes
Baking time: 15 minutes
Yield: 6 servings

Nutrition information per serving:

Calories	325
Fat	14 g
Cholesterol	20 mg
Sodium	170 mg
Carbohydrate	49 g
Protein	5 g

1. Heat oven to 375°F. Place 1 sheet of phyllo dough on a slightly damp towel. Brush lightly with butter. Top with second sheet; repeat buttering and layering remaining phyllo. Brush top sheet with butter; sprinkle with crumbs.

2. Spread fruit over dough. Add sugar, walnuts, and cinnamon. Roll up jelly-roll fashion, using the towel as a guide. Place on a greased 10" × 15" jelly-roll pan. Brush with butter. Bake until golden and crisp, about 12 to 15 minutes. Cool on a wire rack. Serve warm.

Baklava

Preparation time: 1 hour
Baking time: 1½ to 2 hours
Yield: 12 to 14 servings

Nutrition information per serving (based on 12):

Calories	835
Fat	56 g
Cholesterol	80 mg
Sodium	190 mg
Carbohydrate	81 g
Protein	8 g

The good cooks of St. Haralambos Greek Orthodox Church in Chicago divulged cooking secrets during one of their annual Greek food festivals. Katina Vaselopulos, known for her ethereal version of baklava, a walnut torte layered with buttery sheets of phyllo, explained: "Before you put the phyllo in the pan, rumple it slightly. You don't want to flatten the phyllo. That takes the lightness out during baking. You want it to be wrinkled. People think that you can't make baklava ahead of time. You can. Just bake it, cool it, and keep it covered at room temperature. Don't pour the syrup over it until you are ready to serve it. That's the trick."

Baklava
1 16-ounce bag shelled walnuts
¼ cup sugar
1 teaspoon cinnamon
1 pound (4 sticks) unsalted butter
1 16-ounce box frozen phyllo dough, thawed according to
   package directions

Syrup
1½ cups water
3 cups sugar
2 cinnamon sticks
¼ teaspoon whole cloves
Juice and zest from ½ lemon

1. Heat oven to 300°F. Chop nuts in a food processor fitted with a metal blade or in a grinder until finely ground. Mix ground nuts, sugar, and cinnamon in a large bowl. Melt butter in a small saucepan.

2. Lay phyllo dough on a clean towel. Cover with a slightly damp towel. Remove one sheet of dough; put into a buttered 10" × 15" jelly-roll pan. Brush phyllo sheet with butter. Repeat until 5 buttered sheets are in the pan.

3. Sprinkle 1 cup nut mixture over dough. Cover nuts with 1 sheet of phyllo; brush with butter. Sprinkle with 1 cup nut mixture. Repeat layering until nut mixture is gone. Layer remaining phyllo sheets, brushing each with butter. Tuck any overhanging phyllo into the pan. Brush top with remaining butter.

4. Cut through layers with a sharp knife into diamonds before baking. Bake until golden brown and crisp, about 1½ to 2 hours. Cool on a wire rack.

5. For the syrup, put water, sugar, cinnamon sticks, and cloves into a heavy saucepan. Squeeze juice from lemon half into mixture; add lemon zest. Heat to a boil until sugar is dissolved. Reduce heat; simmer, uncovered, 6 minutes. Pour hot syrup slowly over cooled baklava. Cool completely.

Fruit-Filled Hamantaschen

Preparation time: 1 hour

Chilling time: 2 to 3 hours

Cooking time: 10 to 15
    minutes

Yield: About 3 dozen

Nutrition information per cookie:

Calories	95
Fat	4 g
Cholesterol	15 mg
Sodium	55 mg
Carbohydrate	15 g
Protein	1 g

Hadassah Sagalovitch of Chicago sent us her recipe for these traditional Purim cookie/pastries shaped like small tricornered hats. Purim is a festive Jewish holiday; however, these cookies are so good you'll want to make them year-round.

Dough
⅔ cup unsalted butter, softened
½ cup sugar
1 large egg
½ teaspoon pure vanilla extract
3 cups all-purpose flour
1 teaspoon baking powder
Dash salt

Filling
¾ cup pitted prunes, coarsely chopped
⅓ cup dried cherries
¼ cup water
¼ apple, chopped
Zest and juice of ½ lemon

1. For the dough, combine butter and sugar in the large bowl of an electric mixer. Beat on medium speed until light, 2 to 3 minutes. Add egg and vanilla; mix well. Combine flour, baking powder, and salt in a medium bowl. Slowly add to butter mixture, beating well after each addition, until incorporated. Wrap dough in wax paper; chill 2 to 3 hours or overnight.

2. For the filling, heat prunes, cherries, and water to a simmer over medium heat in a small saucepan. Simmer 15 minutes. Remove from heat; stir in apple, lemon zest, and juice. Set aside.

3. Heat oven to 375°F. Divide dough into fourths. Roll each piece out on a floured surface to ⅛-inch thickness. Cut 2½-inch circles out of dough using a cookie cutter. Wet the edge of each circle with water. Drop 1 scant teaspoon filling in the center of each circle. Starting at 3 points equally spaced on each circle, bring the dough from the edge to the center; pinch the 3 edge points together in the center, forming a hat shape.

4. Place on a greased baking sheet. Bake until golden brown, 10 to 15 minutes. Remove to a cooling rack; cool completely.

Sour Cherry Rugelach

Preparation time: 1 hour
Chilling time: 1 hour
Cooking time: 20 minutes
Yield: 64 cookies

Nutrition information per cookie:

Calories	95
Fat	6 g
Cholesterol	17 mg
Sodium	55 mg
Carbohydrate	10 g
Protein	1 g

NOTE
Nuts and cherries are easily chopped, separately, in a food processor. To keep cherries from sticking to the blade, chop with about 1 tablespoon of the sugar.

We loved the sour cherry rugelach that Jean Linsner of Chicago made for the Chicago Tribune *Holiday Cookie Contest. Her first-place effort was a rolled crescent of cream cheese dough filled with spiced, sweet-tart dried cherries and toasted walnuts. Linsner calls her cookies a "12-step program for intimidated would-be bakers." It was so simple to prepare that Linsner—whose previous disaster with a spritz dough had turned her off cookie baking—was lured back to the kitchen. "As these marvels bake," she wrote in her entry letter, "thoughts of sturdy German and Polish grandmas and great-grandmas mingle with the heady aroma of cinnamon and allspice. . . . I am soothed and comforted. What a perfectly lovely thing for a cookie to do." If you can't find dried sour cherries, any other cut-up dried fruits can be used.*

Dough
1 cup (2 sticks) unsalted butter, at room temperature
1 8-ounce package light cream cheese, at room
   temperature
½ cup sugar
2¾ cups all-purpose flour
1 teaspoon salt

Filling
¾ cup sugar
1 3½-ounce package (⅔ cup) dried sour cherries, finely
   chopped
⅔ cup toasted walnuts, finely chopped
½ cup (1 stick) unsalted butter, melted
2 teaspoons ground cinnamon
1 teaspoon ground allspice
⅛ teaspoon salt

Glaze
1 large egg, beaten
Granulated sugar

1. For the dough, beat butter and cream cheese in the large bowl of an electric mixer until light. Add sugar; beat until fluffy. Mix in flour and salt. Gather dough into a ball; gently knead until smooth and flour is incorporated. Divide dough into 8 equal pieces. Flatten into disks; wrap each in plastic wrap. Refrigerate at least 1 hour

2. For the filling, mix sugar, cherries, walnuts, melted butter, cinnamon, allspice, and salt in a medium bowl. Set aside. Heat oven to 350°F.

3. Unwrap dough disks and roll into 8-inch rounds on a lightly floured surface. Spread 3 tablespoons filling onto the center of each dough circle, leaving about a ½-inch border. Cut circle into 8 wedges, using a pizza cutter or other straight blade. Starting at the wide end of each wedge, roll up each cookie tightly. Place tip side down on ungreased cookie sheets; bend into crescents. Repeat with remaining dough disks.

4. Brush each crescent with beaten egg; sprinkle with sugar. Bake until rugelach are golden brown, about 20 minutes. Cool on wire racks.

Tiramisu

Preparation time: 25 minutes
Cooking time: 35 minutes
Chilling time: Overnight
Yield: 6 servings

Nutrition information per serving:

Calories	375
Fat	23 g
Cholesterol	250 mg
Sodium	125 mg
Carbohydrate	35 g
Protein	9 g

Chicago Tribune *columnist Abby Mandel visited a charming rustic country inn, Il Borghetto, in Montefiridolfi, Italy, not far from Florence and came back with this recipe, which was taught there by owner Francesca Cianchi. Tiramisu means "pick me up." This custardlike dessert is best when it has a chance to set up; try to make it at least a day ahead and refrigerate it. You will need a cooking thermometer.*

3 large eggs, separated
6 tablespoons water
8 ounces mascarpone cheese, at room temperature
1 large egg white
½ cup sugar
Pinch salt
14 ladyfingers
1 cup strong rich coffee, cooled
1 tablespoon cognac or brandy
2 tablespoons unsweetened cocoa powder

1. Combine egg yolks and water in a heavy saucepan. Cook over very low heat, whisking constantly, until mixture reaches 160°F on a thermometer, about 15 minutes. Cool quickly in a bowl set over a larger bowl of ice water or in the freezer. Stir mascarpone into yolks.

2. Combine 4 egg whites, sugar, and salt in the top of a double boiler. Cook over very low heat, beating with a hand-held mixer on medium speed or with a whisk until whites hold soft peaks and temperature reaches 160°F, about 20 minutes. Stir ¼ of beaten whites into egg yolk mixture. Fold in remaining whites.

3. To assemble, arrange ladyfingers in a single layer on a piece of heavy-duty foil; slightly turn up foil edges to make a tray. Combine coffee and cognac; drizzle evenly over ladyfingers. Arrange half of ladyfingers in a single layer in a serving dish or bowl, about 6½ inches in diameter and 3 to 4 inches deep. Fill in any spaces with parts of ladyfingers. Cover ladyfinger layer with half of mascarpone mixture. Top with remaining ladyfingers and remaining mascarpone mixture. Cover with plastic wrap. Refrigerate overnight or up to 2 days.

4. Sprinkle cocoa through a fine sieve over surface. Serve chilled.

Fruity Lokshen Kugel

Preparation time: 25 minutes
Cooking time: 45 minutes
Yield: 8 servings

Nutrition information per serving:

Calories	470
Fat	12 g
Cholesterol	95 mg
Sodium	760 mg
Carbohydrate	54 g
Protein	37 g

Each year, at sunset on Yom Kippur, the Day of Atonement, the sounding of the shofar (a ram's horn) signals the end of the Jewish High Holidays and the end of a daylong fast. A favorite sight after fasting all day is the ceremonial table laden with delicious appetizers whose recipes have been passed down from generation to generation. And nearly every table will offer a family recipe for kugel such as this one provided by freelancer Beverly Levitt. The ingredients are rich, but after fasting all day, diners can afford a few extra calories.

Kugel
½ cup raisins
½ cup dried cranberries
1 cup cottage cheese or farmer cheese
1 cup sour cream
2 large eggs, beaten lightly
2 egg whites, beaten lightly
¼ cup packed brown sugar
2 tablespoons melted butter
2 tablespoons honey
1 teaspoon cinnamon
1 teaspoon pure vanilla extract
½ teaspoon salt
1 8-ounce can pineapple tidbits, drained
8 ounces wide egg noodles, cooked and drained

Topping
1 cup crushed corn flakes or raisin bread crumbs
2 tablespoons brown sugar
1 teaspoon cinnamon

1. Heat oven to 350°F. Mix raisins and cranberries in a small bowl; add very hot water to cover; let stand until plumped, about 5 minutes. Drain.

2. Beat cottage cheese, sour cream, eggs, egg whites, brown sugar, butter, honey, cinnamon, vanilla, and salt in the large bowl of an electric mixer until smooth. Add drained raisins, cranberries, and pineapple; blend thoroughly. Add noodles; mix to combine.

3. Turn mixture into a well-buttered 8-inch-square baking dish. Mix topping ingredients together; sprinkle over kugel. Bake until top is browned, about 45 minutes.

Panna Cotta with Caramel Sauce

Preparation time: 25 minutes
Cooking time: 10 minutes
Chilling time: Several hours
Yield: 4 servings

Nutrition information per serving:

Calories	680
Fat	56 g
Cholesterol	210 mg
Sodium	75 mg
Carbohydrate	43 g
Protein	5 g

Panna cotta, a favorite in Piedmont, Italy (which claims to have created it), wins high praise for its elegant simplicity. Literally "cooked cream," a finished dish of panna cotta at first glance resembles Spanish flan and French crème caramel. Upon closer inspection, cooks will notice that panna cotta almost always is eggless and contains little more than cream, sugar, a touch of gelatin, and some flavorings. This recipe is from Coco Pazzo restaurant in the River North neighborhood in Chicago.

1½ teaspoons plain gelatin
2 tablespoons plus ½ cup water
2½ cups whipping cream
½ cup whole milk
½ cup confectioners' sugar
½ vanilla bean, split lengthwise
½ cup granulated sugar
Fresh raspberries, mint sprigs

1. Dissolve gelatin in 2 tablespoons water in a small dish; let stand until softened, about 5 minutes. Heat cream, milk, confectioners' sugar, and vanilla bean in a large, heavy saucepan to a simmer over medium heat. Stir dissolved gelatin into cream. Cook, stirring, just long enough to melt gelatin. Transfer mixture to a stainless steel or glass bowl set in a larger bowl filled with ice. Cool, stirring occasionally, to room temperature. Remove vanilla bean. Divide cream mixture among four 8-ounce molds or custard cups. Refrigerate, covered, for several hours or overnight.

2. For the sauce, combine granulated sugar and ¼ cup water in a small saucepan. Heat to a boil; stir to dissolve sugar. Cover and boil 1 minute. Uncover pan; boil, without stirring, until mixture turns light brown. Very carefully (mixture may spatter) add remaining ¼ cup water; return to a boil. Pour into a small bowl; cool to room temperature.

3. Run a paring knife around the edge of each mold. Invert each onto a serving plate; shake gently to unmold. Pour some caramel sauce over each panna cotta and plate. Garnish with raspberries and mint.

Coffee Crème Brûlée

Preparation time: 20 minutes

Chilling time: 4½ hours

Cooking time: 1½ hours

Yield: 4 servings

Nutrition information per serving:

Calories	430
Fat	37 g
Cholesterol	280 mg
Sodium	85 mg
Carbohydrate	20 g
Protein	7 g

When Debbie Vanni of Libertyville, Illinois, sent us a recipe for the classic English—yes, English, even if the name is French—crème brûlée flavored with espresso, any notions about low-fat eating flew right out the window. We reveled in the rich taste and sublime texture, toasted our indulgence, and then vowed to behave for the rest of the day.

1½ cups whipping cream

¼ cup granulated sugar

¾ teaspoon instant espresso coffee powder

1 teaspoon pure vanilla extract

3 large egg yolks

2 tablespoons packed brown sugar

1. Heat oven to 325°F. Set four 6-ounce soufflé dishes, ramekins, or custard cups into a shallow roasting pan large enough to hold the dishes. Heat a kettle of water to a boil; keep hot.

2. Mix cream, granulated sugar, and ½ teaspoon espresso powder in a small saucepan or a 4-cup microwave-safe measuring cup. Heat until sugar and espresso dissolve; do not boil. Remove from heat; stir in vanilla.

3. Whisk egg yolks in a medium bowl. Add cream mixture; whisk lightly, just until combined. Pour mixture into soufflé dishes, not quite filling to the top. Transfer the pan to an oven rack and pour boiling water into the roasting pan until the water comes halfway up the sides of the soufflé dishes.

4. Bake until the custard is softly set in the center, about 1½ hours. Remove the dishes from hot water; let cool on a cooling rack. Refrigerate 4 hours or overnight.

5. About 30 minutes before serving, heat broiler. Mix brown sugar and remaining ¼ teaspoon espresso powder in a small bowl. Sprinkle evenly over custards. Broil until sugar melts and caramelizes, 40 to 60 seconds, watching constantly so topping doesn't burn. Refrigerate about 30 minutes.

Peasant Apple Bread Pudding

Preparation time: 25 minutes
Cooking time: 1 hour
Yield: 8 servings

Nutrition information per serving:

Calories	300
Fat	15 g
Cholesterol	195 mg
Sodium	160 mg
Carbohydrate	34 g
Protein	7 g

Bread pudding is a multinational treat Chicago Tribune *staff writer Lisa Anderson discovered during a reporting trip to Italy in 1993. In the Alto Adige region, at the foot of the Alps across the border from Austria, she tasted this delicious version of the dessert, which contains apple, yogurt, and the addictive sweet cheese called mascarpone. It's easy to make in any language.*

½ cup mascarpone cheese, at room temperature
½ cup plus 2 tablespoons sugar
5 large egg yolks
1½ cups whole milk
1 8-ounce carton plain yogurt
Zest of 1 lemon
1 teaspoon pure vanilla extract
6 ¾-inch-thick slices day-old French or Italian bread
2 McIntosh apples, peeled, cored, and sliced
2 tablespoons unsalted butter, cut into small pieces

1. Heat oven to 325°F. Stir mascarpone cheese and ½ cup sugar together in a large bowl. Add egg yolks; mix lightly. Whisk in milk, yogurt, lemon zest, and vanilla.

2. Layer bread and apples in a buttered 6-cup gratin or shallow baking dish. Pour cheese mixture over. Dot with butter pieces; sprinkle with remaining 2 tablespoons sugar. Bake just until set, 50 to 60 minutes. Serve warm or at room temperature.

Chocolate Mousse

Chef-caterer James Boardman of Chicago shared this mouthwatering recipe for one of France's most famous desserts. It was served at a festive 1991 open house in the Beverly neighborhood to benefit the Chicago Child Care Society.

2 cups whipping cream
1 cup whole milk
¼ cup sugar
6 ounces semisweet chocolate, finely chopped
8 large egg yolks, lightly beaten
½ cup confectioners' sugar
1½ teaspoons cognac
1½ teaspoons pure vanilla extract

1. Heat 1 cup cream and the milk and sugar to a boil in a medium saucepan over medium heat. Remove from heat; add chocolate, whisking until smooth. Add egg yolks; cook gently, stirring constantly, until slightly thickened, 3 to 4 minutes. Strain through a fine mesh strainer. Refrigerate until well chilled, about 2 hours.

2. Whip remaining 1 cup cream until soft peaks form. Mix in confectioners' sugar, cognac, and vanilla. Gently fold into cooled chocolate mixture. Refrigerate until set, 2 to 3 hours or as long as 2 days before serving.

Preparation time: 20 minutes
Cooking time: 5 minutes
Chilling time: 4 hours or overnight
Yield: About 5 cups

Nutrition information per cup:

Calories	710
Fat	55 g
Cholesterol	480 mg
Sodium	75 mg
Carbohydrate	49 g
Protein	9 g

Easter Cheese Dessert

Preparation time: 1 hour

Chilling time: About 24 hours

Yield: 32 servings

Nutrition information per serving:

Calories	430
Fat	36 g
Cholesterol	110 mg
Sodium	300 mg
Carbohydrate	14 g
Protein	11 g

Nancy Melvin shared this recipe for her grandmother's paskha, the cheesecake-like Russian dessert that is made in a traditional pyramid-shaped wooden mold (or in 8-inch-diameter clay flowerpots with holes in the bottoms). This dessert is traditionally served as part of the Russian Orthodox Easter feast.

3 pounds farmer cheese, at room temperature

1 pound (4 sticks) unsalted butter, softened

1 quart (4 cups) whipping cream

2 cups sugar

1 vanilla bean, cut into fourths lengthwise

2 eggs, beaten

2 to 3 tablespoons rum

1 cup (4 ounces) slivered almonds, lightly toasted

1. Combine cheese and egg whites in a large bowl. Transfer mixture to a colander lined with cheesecloth, set over a bowl. Place a weight on top, such as 28-ounce cans; let drain in refrigerator overnight. (Mixture must be very dry.)

2. Push mixture through a fine wire mesh strainer; discard liquid. Beat mixture together with butter in the large bowl of an electric mixer until smooth. Set aside.

3. Heat cream, sugar, and vanilla bean in a medium saucepan over low heat, stirring frequently, 30 minutes. Stir small amount of mixture into eggs. Pour egg mixture into saucepan; cook, stirring, until thick, about 10 minutes. Be careful not to burn mixture. Cool quickly by placing the saucepan in a bowl of ice water, stirring until cooled. Remove vanilla bean; stir in rum. Stir cream mixture into cheese mixture. Fold in almonds.

4. Rinse three layers of cheesecloth in cold water. Line a mold with holes in the bottom or a flowerpot with cheesecloth, leaving some to hang over the sides. Place mixture into mold or pot; fold edges of cheesecloth over mixture. Place a small plate on top of mixture; put a heavy weight on top of the plate. Place the mold or pot into a dish with sides. Refrigerate 12 hours. Discard liquid as it accumulates in the bottom of the dish.

5. Unmold cheese mixture by gently tapping mold onto serving plate. Decorate as desired. Slice and serve, or spread on sweet bread.

Dried-Fruit Compote

Preparation time: 5 minutes

Cooking time: 20 minutes

Yield: 6 cups

Nutrition information per cup:

Calories	440
Fat	1 g
Cholesterol	0 mg
Sodium	30 mg
Carbohydrate	115 g
Protein	3 g

Barbara Mirecki of Chicago contributed this easy-to-prepare fruit compote from Poland to a Chicago Tribune Magazine *feature on favorite holiday treats from fourteen cultures. Use your favorite dried fruits such as apricots, apples, or prunes. Serve it by itself or with cookies, poppy seed cake, or spice cake.*

1½ pounds mixed dried fruit

6 cups water

8 whole cloves

2 long strips lemon rind, removed with vegetable peeler

3 whole allspice

1 stick cinnamon

1¼ cups sugar or to taste

1. Put all ingredients in a 3-quart nonaluminum saucepan. Heat to a boil; reduce heat. Simmer until fruit is soft and water is syrupy, about 20 minutes. Cool; refrigerate at least 4 hours.

Vanilla and Rum–Spiced Pineapple

Vanilla is one of Mexico's great gifts to world cuisine. Chicago Tribune food writer Pat Dailey used it and other tropical flavorings to make this almost instant fruit and rum dessert or daytime refreshment for her "Fast Food" column. In some supermarkets, fresh pineapple may be purchased already peeled and cored, which cuts the preparation time considerably.

1¼ cups water

⅓ cup sugar

1 vanilla bean, split lengthwise

1 cinnamon stick

¼ teaspoon anise seeds

3 tablespoons dark rum

Juice of ½ lime

1 fresh pineapple, peeled and cut in chunks

1. Combine water, sugar, vanilla bean, cinnamon stick, and anise seeds in a medium saucepan. Heat to a boil; cook 1 minute.

2. Remove from heat; add rum and lime juice. Stir in pineapple. Fruit may be chilled for several hours or overnight or served at room temperature.

Preparation time: 15 minutes

Cooking time: 5 minutes

Yield: 4 servings

Nutrition information per serving:

Calories	150
Fat	0.5 g
Cholesterol	0 mg
Sodium	4 mg
Carbohydrate	32 g
Protein	0.5 g

Swedish Spice Cookies

Preparation time: 45 minutes

Cooking time: 9 to 10
   minutes per batch

Yield: About 5 dozen

Des Plaines, Illinois, high school student Colleen Ries won the Chicago Tribune's eighth annual Good Eating Holiday Cookie Contest in 1995 with Swedish spice cookies. The recipe came from her grandmother, who taught Ries how to bake and decorate cookies. Delightfully chewy and delicious, these can be left plain, decorated, or glazed as desired.

Nutrition information per cookie:

Calories	75
Fat	2 g
Cholesterol	10 mg
Sodium	80 mg
Carbohydrate	13 g
Protein	1 g

2¼ cups sifted all-purpose flour
2 teaspoons baking soda
1 teaspoon ground cloves
1 teaspoon ginger
1 teaspoon cinnamon
1 teaspoon salt
¾ cup (1½ sticks) unsalted butter, at room temperature
1½ cups sugar
1 large egg
¼ cup molasses

1. Heat oven to 375°F. Sift flour, baking soda, spices, and salt together in a medium bowl; set aside. Beat butter and 1 cup sugar in the large bowl of an electric mixer on high speed until light, 1 minute. Add egg and molasses; mix well. Add flour mixture. Mix just until combined.

2. Using about 1½ teaspoons dough for each, roll dough into balls. Roll balls in remaining ½ cup sugar to fully coat. Arrange on ungreased baking sheets, spacing 2 inches apart. If a thin, crisp cookie is preferred, flatten with the bottom of a glass that has been dipped in sugar. Bake until set, 9 to 10 minutes. Transfer to a wire rack; cool.

Greek Almond Shortbread Cookies

Bess Gallanis Hayes of Winnetka, Illinois, entered these delicious Greek almond shortbread cookies in the Chicago Tribune 1996 Good Eating Holiday Cookie Contest, *where they received an honorable mention.*

Preparation time: 1 hour

Baking time: 15 minutes per batch

Yield: About 4 dozen

½ cup blanched almonds
1 pound (4 sticks) unsalted butter, at room temperature
1 1-pound box confectioners' sugar
2 large egg yolks
3 tablespoons brandy or cognac
1 teaspoon pure vanilla extract
3 cups cake flour
½ teaspoon baking powder

Nutrition information per cookie:

Calories	135
Fat	9 g
Cholesterol	30 mg
Sodium	7 mg
Carbohydrate	14 g
Protein	1 g

1. Heat oven to 350°F. Spread almonds in a single layer on a baking sheet. Bake, stirring occasionally, until lightly toasted, about 10 minutes. Remove from oven; cool. Chop coarsely.

2. Beat butter in the large bowl of an electric mixer on medium-high speed until very light and fluffy, 5 minutes. Add 3 tablespoons confectioners' sugar; continue beating 3 minutes. Add egg yolks, brandy, and vanilla; beat until smooth. Beat in almonds, flour, and baking powder until mixed well. (If dough is too soft to handle, add additional flour.)

3. Shape 1 tablespoon dough per cookie between palms into round balls or crescents. Place on ungreased baking sheets. Bake until set and very pale golden, about 15 minutes. Remove cookies to a wire rack.

4. Place remaining confectioners' sugar into a sifter. While cookies are still hot, sift confectioners' sugar over tops. Repeat two more times at 20-minute intervals.

Mexican Pecan Cookies

Preparation time: 45 minutes

Baking time: 22 to 25 minutes
per batch

Yield: About 3 dozen

Nutrition information per cookie:

Calories	110
Fat	7 g
Cholesterol	16 mg
Sodium	30 mg
Carbohydrate	12 g
Protein	1 g

Third-place winner in the Chicago Tribune's *1996 Good Eating Holiday Cookie Contest was Marilyn Cahill of Chicago. She learned the recipe during a visit to the home of Eva Trejo. "Because Mrs. Trejo had fewer modern appliances than I am used to, I resorted to the old pecans-in-a-plastic-bag crushed-by-a-hammer and beating 300 strokes, with me counting in Spanish and Mrs. Trejo practicing her English numbers. Try doing that without having a few laughs."*

1 cup sugar
½ cup (1 stick) unsalted butter, at room temperature
1 large egg yolk
1 teaspoon pure vanilla extract
2¼ cups all-purpose flour
¾ teaspoon cinnamon
¼ teaspoon anise seed, finely crushed
Pinch salt
½ cup finely chopped pecans

1. Heat oven to 325°F. Beat ¾ cup sugar and the butter in the large bowl of an electric mixer on high speed until light and fluffy, about 3 minutes. Add egg yolk and vanilla; beat until smooth. Beat in flour, cinnamon, anise seed, and salt until well mixed. Stir in pecans.

2. Roll walnut-sized pieces of dough between palms to make round balls. Put remaining ¼ cup sugar in a pie plate; roll dough balls in sugar. Place balls 5 inches apart on un-greased cookie sheets. Press each ball with the bottom of a glass dipped in sugar to about ¼-inch thickness. Bake until set and bottoms are barely golden, 22 to 25 minutes per batch. Cool on a wire rack.

Shortbread Cookies

It doesn't take much—except talent—to create a prize-winning cookie, Sandra Petrille of Naperville, Illinois, discovered when her simple, three-ingredient Scottish shortbread won second prize in a *Good Eating* Holiday Cookie Contest. She wrote, "This recipe is so easy I hesitate to enter it. I guess easy can be a big advantage, though, when we are so busy getting ready for Christmas."

4 cups all-purpose flour
1 cup packed light-brown sugar
1 pound (4 sticks) unsalted butter, at room temperature

1. Heat oven to 325°F. Beat all ingredients in the large bowl of an electric mixer on medium-high speed until smooth, about 4 minutes.

2. Divide dough into 4 pieces. Roll out 1 piece of dough at a time on a lightly floured surface to 1/16- to 1/8-inch thickness. Cut out dough with cookie cutters.

3. Bake cookies on ungreased baking sheets until pale brown and slightly firm to the touch, 8 to 10 minutes. Cool on a wire rack.

Preparation time: 25 minutes
Baking time: 8 to 10 minutes
 per batch
Yield: About 4 dozen

Nutrition information per cookie:

Calories	115
Fat	8 g
Cholesterol	20 mg
Sodium	80 mg
Carbohydrate	11 g
Protein	1 g

Caramel Oat Bars

Preparation time: 20 minutes
Cooking time: 30 minutes
Yield: 16 bars

Nutrition information per bar:

Calories	300
Fat	17 g
Cholesterol	50 mg
Sodium	180 mg
Carbohydrate	35 g
Protein	3 g

In the highly competitive Chicago Tribune *1996 Good Eating Holiday Cookie Contest, even the honorable mentions were worth noting. Therefore, we published this simple but very pleasing English recipe for caramel oat bars from Karen Kruckenberg of Harvard, Illinois.*

Base
½ cup (1 stick) unsalted butter, at room temperature
¼ cup sugar
¾ cup rolled oats
⅔ cup all-purpose flour

Caramel
1 14-ounce can sweetened condensed milk
½ cup (1 stick) unsalted butter
¼ cup packed brown sugar
1 to 2 teaspoons pure vanilla extract

Icing
¼ cup (½ stick) unsalted butter
2 tablespoons sifted cocoa
2 tablespoons water
1½ cups confectioners' sugar, sifted

1. Heat oven to 350°F. For the base, beat butter and sugar in the small bowl of an electric mixer on medium-high speed until light and fluffy, 3 minutes. Add oats and flour; beat until smooth. Press into a greased 8-inch square baking pan. Bake until set, about 20 minutes.

2. For the caramel mixture, heat condensed milk, butter, and brown sugar to a boil in a heavy saucepan over medium heat. Boil, stirring constantly, 5 minutes. Remove from heat; stir in vanilla. Pour caramel mixture over cooked base; allow to cool completely.

3. For icing, melt butter in a saucepan over medium heat. Stir in cocoa and water until smooth. Add confectioners' sugar; stir until well mixed. Spread over cooled caramel layer. Allow to set before cutting. Store in refrigerator.

Appendix

Fiore's Imported & Domestic Food, Near West Side

Ethnic Markets

The following are just some of the many ethnic markets in the Chicago area that are a source for meat, fish, groceries, and produce. The markets are grouped by geographic region and by country within a region. Descriptions of the markets have been added, when necessary, to clarify store products or to highlight special services. When "mail order" is indicated, the store will ship requested items to your home, even though it does not have catalogs per se. Many markets have similar product lines; you may find Hungarian sausage, for instance, at a German store.

The following markets are in Chicago unless otherwise noted. Please note that the information is subject to change.

African and Caribbean

CARIBBEAN AMERICAN BAKING CO.
1539 W. Howard St.
773-761-0700

OLD WORLD MARKET
5129 N. Broadway
773-989-4440
African, Jamaican, and Caribbean foods.

Asian

General Asian

DIHO MARKET
International Plaza
665 Pasquinelli Dr.
Westmont
630-323-1668
Full-service, supermarket-sized store.

YOUNG'S FISH MARKET
3539 W. Lawrence Ave.
773-539-3122
Fresh and frozen fish and shellfish; sushi and sashimi.

Chinese

DONG KEE CO.
2252 S. Wentworth Ave.
312-225-6340

GOLDEN COUNTRY ORIENTAL FOOD CO.
2422 S. Wentworth Ave.
312-842-4111
Groceries, roasted meats.

THE ORIENTAL FOOD MARKET AND COOKING SCHOOL
2801 W. Howard St.
773-274-2826
Asian foodstuffs, cooking equipment, porcelain. Mail order.

Filipino

R&E Oriental Foods
133 W. Prospect Ave.
Mt. Prospect
847-253-4339
Delivery available for orders of $50 or more.

Indian/Pakistani

Bangla Bazaar
2321 W. Devon Ave.
773-262-3500
Fresh fish imported from Bangladesh.

Jai Hind
2658 W. Devon Ave.
773-973-3400
Full grocery store, dine-in and take-out.

Patel Brothers
2610 W. Devon Ave.
773-262-7777

Suchir
661 N. Cass Ave.
Westmont
630-920-0115

Japanese

Koyama
256 E. Algonquin Rd.
Arlington Heights
847-228-5544

Sea Ranch
1087 E. Golf Rd.
Arlington Heights
847-956-7040
Groceries and fresh seafood.

Yaohan Plaza
100 E. Algonquin Rd.
Arlington Heights
847-956-6699
Shopping center with everything from take-out sushi to sweets and housewares.

Korean

Arirang Super Market
4017 W. Lawrence Ave.
773-777-2400

Clark Market
4853–55 N. Kedzie Ave.
773-478-2262
Groceries and take-out meals.

Dong-A Food
3933 W. Touhy Ave.
Lincolnwood
847-673-3055

Thai

Asian World Food
217 National St.
Elgin
847-888-2201
Thai groceries and some Filipino products.

THAI GROCERY
5014 N. Broadway
773-561-5345
Fresh meat and fish, groceries, cookware.

THAILAND PLAZA
4821 N. Broadway
773-728-1199
*Groceries, cookware, and Thai cookbooks
(some in English).*

Vietnamese/Cambodian/ Other Southeast Asian

HOA NAM MARKET
1101 W. Argyle St.
773-275-9157
Vietnamese and Asian groceries.

KHMER FOOD STORE
1116 W. Leland Ave.
773-728-2753
Cambodian and Asian groceries.

MIEN HOA
1108 W. Argyle St.
773-334-8393
*Vietnamese, Chinese, and Cambodian
groceries.*

TAI NAM
4925 N. Broadway
773-275-5666.

TRUNG VIET CO.
4940 N. Sheridan Rd.
773-561-0042

VIET HOA PLAZA
1051 W. Argyle St.
773-334-1028
Vietnamese and Cambodian groceries.

European
British

BRITISH ACCENTS INC.
116 Old McHenry Rd.
Long Grove
847-913-0855
Packaged goods from England. Mail order.

GAELIC IMPORTS
4736 N. Austin Ave.
773-545-6515
Packaged and prepared Irish foods.

WINSTON'S
4701 W. 63rd St.
773-767-4353
7959 W. 159th St.
Tinley Park
708-633-7500
*Specialty meats, packaged goods from Ireland,
England, Scotland. Mail order available from
Tinley Park location.*

German

DELICATESSEN MEYER
4750 N. Lincoln Ave.
773-561-3377
Sausage and other meat products. Mail order.

KUHN'S DELICATESSEN
116 S. Waukegan Rd.
Deerfield
847-272-4197
749 W. Golf Rd.
Des Plaines
847-640-0222
Mail order.

PAULINA MARKET
3501 N. Lincoln Ave.
773-248-6272
Meat, sausages, prepared food. Mail order.

Greek

ATHENS GROCERY
324 S. Halsted St.
312-332-6737
Cheeses, olives, wines, and assorted packaged goods.

DELPHI FOOD MARKET
2655 W. Lawrence Ave.
773-271-0660
Assorted packaged goods.

MEDITERRANEAN DELI
1805 S. Wolf Rd.
Hillside
708-449-2030
Specialty Greek foods prepared on premises, cheeses, meats, fresh phyllo, packaged foods.

OLYMPIA FOODS
10650 S. Roberts Rd.
Palos Hills
708-974-1212
Deli with imported cheeses and olives, assorted packaged goods.

Hungarian

BENDE INC.
925 Corporate Woods Pkwy.
Vernon Hills
847-913-0304
Cured and smoked meats, pickles, peppers, paprika, honey, noodles. Mail order.

EUROPEAN SAUSAGE HOUSE
4361 N. Lincoln Ave.
773-472-9645

JOE'S
4452 N. Western Ave.
773-478-5443
Mail order.

LALICH DELICATESSEN
4208 W. Lawrence Ave.
773-545-3642
Salami, peppers, pickles.

Italian

ANGELO CAPUTO'S
2560 N. Harlem Ave.
Elmwood Park
708-453-0155
240 W. Lake St.
Addison
630-543-0151
1250 Lake St.
Hanover Park
630-372-2800
Produce and packaged goods.

ASTI ITALIAN FOODS
1213 W. Irving Park Rd.
Bensenville
630-350-1874

BACIO ITALIAN FOODS
424 N. Sheridan Rd.
Highwood
847-432-1090

CALABRIA IMPORTS
13012 S. Western Ave.
Blue Island
708-388-1500
Mail order.

CONTE DI SAVOIA
1438 W. Taylor St.
312-666-3471
Mail order.

FRANGELLA ITALIAN IMPORTS
11901 S. 80th Ave.
Palos Park
708-448-2598
Mail order.

GINO'S ITALIAN IMPORTS
3420 N. Harlem Ave.
773-745-8310

L'APPETITO
John Hancock Building
875 N. Michigan Ave.
312-337-0691
30 E. Huron St.
312-787-9881
Mail order.

PASTA FRESH
3418 N. Harlem Ave.
773-745-5888
Specializes in all types of pasta.

THE PASTA SHOPPE AND ITALIAN DELI
3755 N. Harlem Ave.
773-736-7477
Mail order.

PASTIFICIO!
122 Highwood Ave.
Highwood
847-520-7784
Northern Italian products. Mail order.

RUBINO'S ITALIAN IMPORTS
16740 Oak Park Ave.
Tinley Park
708-614-0755

VALLI PRODUCE
450 E. Golf Rd.
Arlington Heights
847-439-9700

Jewish/Kosher

EBNER'S KOSHER MEAT MARKET
2649 W. Devon Ave.
773-764-1446

GOOD MORGAN KOSHER FISH
MARKET
2948 W. Devon Ave.
773-764-8115
Mail order.

KOL TUV KOSHER FOODS
2938 W. Devon Ave.
773-764-1800
Imported kosher wines, kosher health food.

KOSHER KARRY
2828 W. Devon Ave.
773-973-4355

MILLER'S KOSHER MEAT MARKET
2727 W. Devon Ave.
773-761-2168
Custom cuts, glatt kosher meat. Mail order within Illinois only.

NEW YORK KOSHER
2900 W. Devon Ave.
773-338-3354

Polish

CAESAR'S POLISH DELI
901 N. Damen Ave.
773-486-6190
Mail order.

E&J DELI
6556 W. 79th St.
Burbank
708-598-1121
Beer, vodkas, and syrup flavorings.

JOE AND FRANK'S FAMOUS
HOMEMADE SAUSAGE
8720 S. Ridgeland Ave.
Oak Lawn
708-599-3800

KALINOWSKI'S HOMEMADE
SAUSAGE SHOP
5930 W. Lawrence Ave.
773-282-6988

STAROPOLSKA RESTAURANT AND DELI
3028 N. Milwaukee Ave.
773-342-0779

TERESA'S DELI
3184 N. Milwaukee Ave.
773-282-5515

VICTOR'S EUROPEAN SAUSAGE SHOP
5952 W. Lawrence Ave.
773-286-4230
Mail order.

Russian/Former Soviet States

ANN'S BAKERY
2158 W. Chicago Ave.
773-384-5562
Ukrainian baked goods.

GLOBUS DELICATESSEN
2909 W. Devon Ave.
773-973-7970
Meats, prepared foods.

KASHTAN DELICATESSEN
2740 W. Devon Ave.
773-338-9080
Meats, prepared foods.

TALMAN GROCERY AND DELI
2624 W. 69th St.
773-434-9766
Lithuanian prepared foods and meats.

THREE SISTERS DELICATESSEN
2854 W. Devon Ave.
773-973-1919
Meats, prepared foods.

Swedish

ERICKSON'S DELICATESSEN AND

FISH MARKET
5250 N. Clark St.
773-561-5634
Mail order.

HAGEN'S FISH MARKET
5635 W. Montrose Ave.
773-283-1944
Swedish and Polish prepared foods, smoked and pickled fish, lutefisk, lefse.

WIKSTROM'S GOURMET FOODS AND CATERING
5247 N. Clark St.
773-275-6100
Meatballs, potato sausage, and herring. Mail order.

Mediterranean and Middle Eastern

AL-KHYAM MEAT, BAKERY AND GROCERY
4738 N. Kedzie Ave.
773-583-3099
Mail order.

COLUMBUS FOOD MARKET & BAKERY
1651 Rand Rd.
Des Plaines
847-297-6660
Mail order.

FARM CITY MEAT
2255 W. Devon Ave.
773-274-2255

Farm Meat Market
4810 N. Kedzie Ave.
773-588-1266
Halal meats.

Holy Land Bakery and Grocery
Store
4806 N. Kedzie Ave.
773-588-3306

International Grocery and
Meat Market
8747 S. Ridgeland Ave.
Oak Lawn
708-233-9999

Middle Eastern Bakery
and Grocery
1512 W. Foster Ave.
773-561-2224
Mail order.

Zabiha Meat Market
2907 W. Devon
773-274-6700
Halal meats.

Mexican/Central and South American

Andy's Fruit Ranch
4725 N. Kedzie Ave.
773-583-2322
Unusual fruits and groceries.

Armando's
2627 S. Kedzie Ave.
773-927-6688
5644 W. Cermak Rd.
Cicero
708-656-9002
Mexican hot sauces, produce.

Carniceria Atotonilco
3917 W. 26th St.
773-521-7077
Fresh meats.

El Guero No. 4
9029 S. Commercial Ave.
773-978-4981
Mexican groceries.

El Paso Carniceria
508 Grove St.
Aurora
630-851-5010
632 E. New York Ave.
Aurora
630-898-6639
Mexican produce, groceries.

Fruteria and Carniceria
La Huerta
1759 W. 18th St.
312-733-0883
Mexican supermarket.

JIMENEZ
3850 W. Fullerton Ave.
773-278-6769
Mexican and Latin groceries.

JOE'S FRUIT MARKET
12958 S. Western Ave.
Blue Island
708-371-5990
Mexican produce.

LA JUSTICIA
3644 W. 26th St.
773-277-8120
Mexican and South American items.

SUPERMERCADO PANAMERICANO
5647 N. Clark St.
773-275-7474
Groceries from North, Central, and South America.

Index